# RETROSPECT

*Aldershot to Damascus, a story of WW1*

By G.E. Badcock
& H. Austwick

Text copyright © 2020 Henry Austwick
All Rights Reserved
First Published 2020
Maps by: Annabel Hewitson
Cover design and Colourisation by Joshua Barrett joshuatobiasbarrett.co.uk
Typesetting by: sam stone (www.samstone.me)
ISBN: 978-1-9163344-1-0

# CONTENTS

| | |
|---|---|
| Preface | 1 |
| Maps | 4 |
| The Author | 7 |
| The Army Service Corps | 9 |
| Other Campaigns & The Enemy | 11 |
| Abbreviations | 12 |

## RETROSPECT
| | |
|---|---|
| Aldershot | 13 |
| Gallipoli | 17 |
| Egypt | 35 |
| Palestine | 45 |
| Damascus | 67 |
| Jerusalem | 77 |
| Afterwards | 83 |

## APPENDIX
| | |
|---|---|
| About the Author & his world | 87 |
| The Army Service Corps | 93 |
| Other Campaigns | 99 |
| The Ottoman Empire | 100 |
| Timeline | 103 |
| Badcock's Narrative of Events | 108 |
| *(from 24th April 1915- Landing on W.Beach)* | |
| Bibliography | 113 |

45, GEORGE STREET,
EDINBURGH.

24th August, 1955

Brigadier G.E. Badcock, CBE., DSO.,
Lobwood,
Blagdon Hill,
Taunton.
Som.

Dear Brigadier Badcock,

Thank you for your very nice letter of 20th August, and also for letting me see "Retrospect". I found this an attractively written paper and I certainly had no difficulty in reading it, but I am afraid I must say that I cannot use it in Maga. Although I have no doubt that it would appeal to the older generation of readers I feel the majority would think there was no real reason for bringing up the 1914-18 War now.

Believe me I am sorry that I have to return this manuscript to you, but I hope you will try again with something a little more up to date, and that eventually you will become a contributor as well as a subscriber.

If you happen to see him, please give my regards to Captain Withinshaw. I knew him well when I was Commanding the Aerodrome at Culmhead during the war.

Yours sincerely,

G.I. Blackwood

## Preface

The journey of getting to this moment has been much longer than I first thought or even believed. The original manuscript for Retrospect was first rediscovered back in 2009.

Discovered in an old box in the loft of my Grandmother's house was my Great Grandfather's handwritten retrospective account of the time he served in the Middle East during the First World War. In a neat Copperplate font as clear as the day he sat down to write it, was the simple title, 'Retrospect'.

Written in 1955, it has taken until now for this personal and humorous account to make it into a book. Why? There are too many reasons to cite; however, a covering letter attached to the original manuscript helps provide an answer. The letter is from a G.D. Blackwood, a publisher and editor:

"The majority of readers would think there was no real reason for bringing up the 1914-18 War."

This may have been true in the 1950s but certainly not true for today. Another common theme which has been bought to light over the last 100 years, as we remember those who fell and those who survived, lies in numbers "Unlike British Armies in France, we were not a gigantic force; we only dealt in thousands, where France dealt in millions".

# RETROSPECT

In "A History of The Transport Services of The Egyptian Expeditionary Force 1916-1918", G.E. Badcock called that Front 'a side show in it's day and by some, considered to be an 'easy war'.

The campaign itself encompassed vast distances and different terrain - from deserts to mountains, oases to cities. This wide range of environments led to other problems, lack of water & food, practical isolation from other forces & resources and the opposition of a brutal enemy.

One Commander of the Egyptian Expeditionary Force, Lord Allenby stated "Seldom if ever, can the Royal Army Service Corps have been confronted with problems so difficult as those which called for solution during the advance of the Expeditionary Force through Palestine and Syria in 1917-18. Deserts, morasses, hills, valleys, rocks and rugged mountains, all had to be conquered; while climatic conditions included extremes of heat and cold, of drought and torrential rain."

He himself had served on the Western Front and was at heart a Cavalry Commander. More on him later.

The reasons for his statement now become elementary and possibly a subject for another book in itself. This book is not a serious 'historical textbook, neither is it pure primary archive material', it is a mix and match of all the information that is to hand.

Readers familiar with WW1 and especially those familiar with the War in the Middle East, will notice early on, that there is little mention of the Arab Revolt or T.E. Lawrence. This is deliberate and in no way intended to undermine the importance of the revolt or of Lawrence's work in fighting the Turks, but they have little direct influence on the story to be told here.

It is easy, especially with WW1, to view each theatre in isolation, the events on one Front had an impact on another.

After all there was not an unlimited number of troops or resources on either side. For example, in early 1918 a major German Offensive on the Western Front saw the British and Commonwealth advance stalled as the E.E.F. was drained of it best troops.

A final note on this book- the original Retrospect manuscript is not written in chronological order, the events that happened are out of sync but to preserve its story, I have kept it in the order it was written so our story flows as it was intended.

In the main text Badcock's words are as written and have been printed in a different font and Italicised.

This is a story, the story of one man, the people he met, the things he did and witnessed.

The campaigns in Sinai, Palestine & Mesopotamia have had long lasting effects on both the region and the rest of the World, starting with the Mandate period and going on to the creation of the State of Israel and Jordan, effects that we still see and feel today.

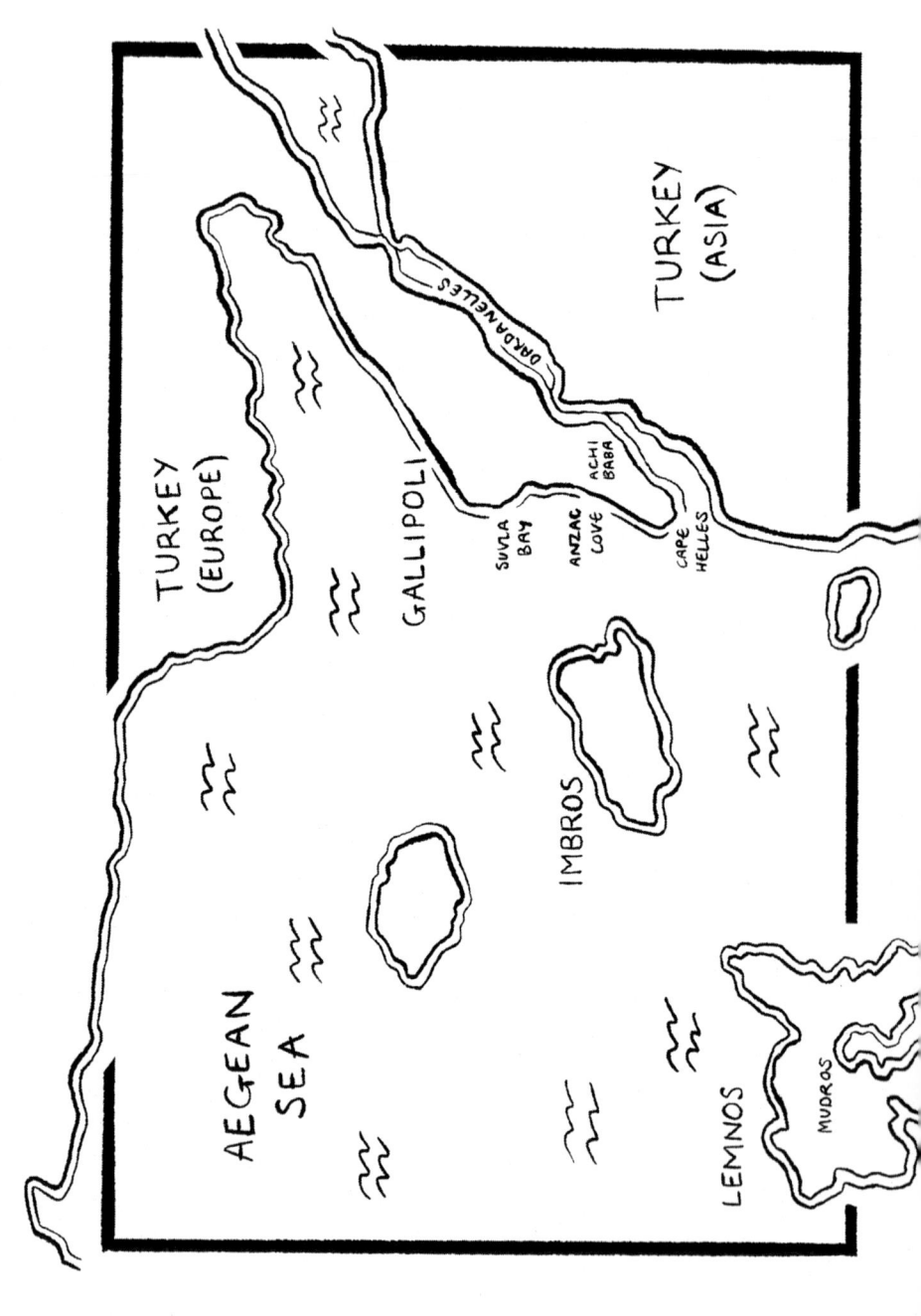

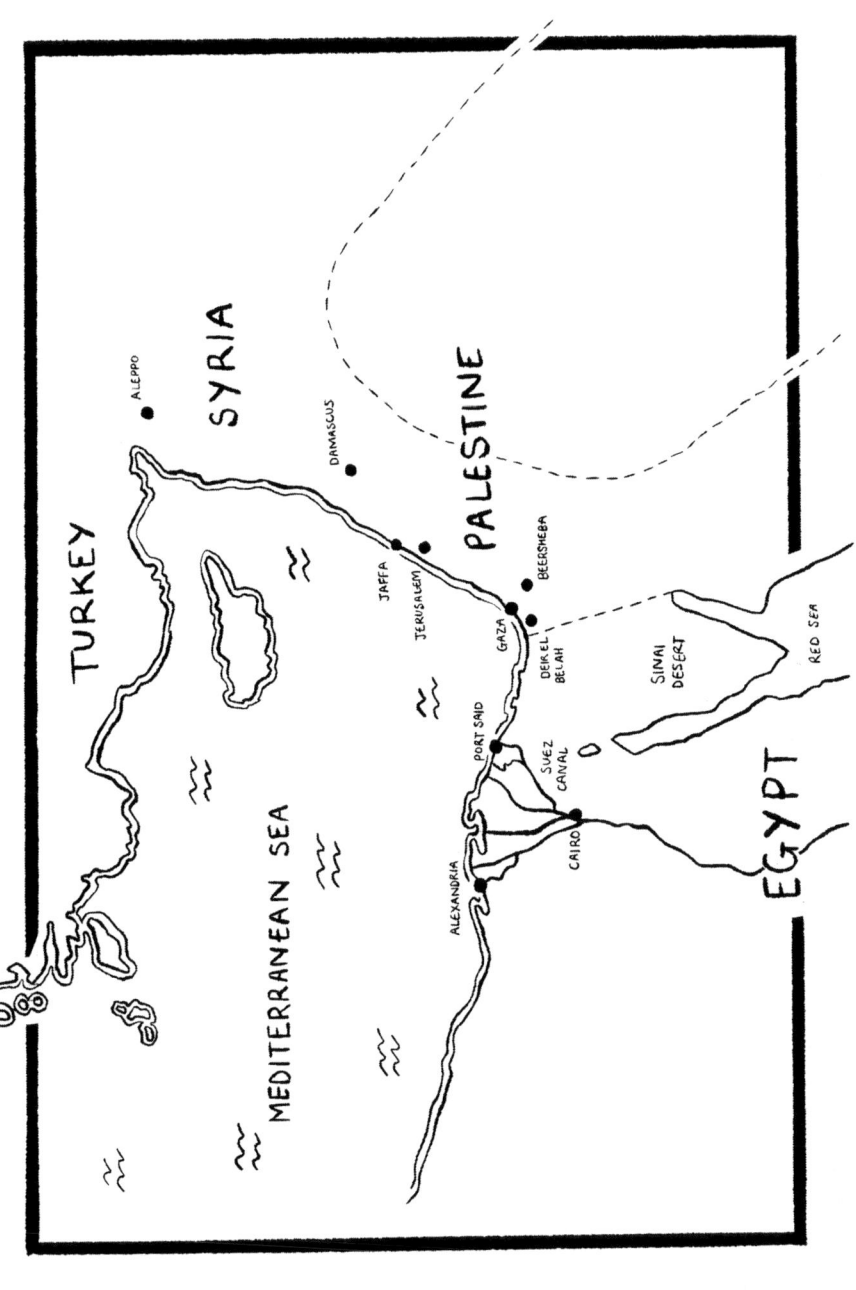

Gerald Eliot Badcock

## THE AUTHOR

### A brief note

Gerald Eliot Badcock, did not set out to be a soldier, he in fact wanted to be a doctor. Fate had other ideas and he joined the army in 1904. At the outbreak of the First World War he found himself at Aldershot (home of the British Army) before setting sail to Gallipoli then onwards to North Africa and the Middle East.

Jump to the Appendix for a fuller account of his life, before, during and after the War.

# RETROSPECT

Army Service Corps illustration by R Pooley

## ARMY SERVICE CORPS

Another brief note...

The histories of great wars are concentrated on the doings of the fighting troops who took part therein: here and there mention is made of transport or supplies *"... there is no glamour attached to them, their work is taken for granted and they seldom, if ever, appear in the limelight of history, unless, through their breakdown, some first-class catastrophe occurs!"*
- Badcock

An army marches on its stomach and you can have the finest troops in the World, but unless they are supplied with food, drink, equipment and transport, they quickly become almost useless. The role of the Army Service Corps (ASC) was this and more besides. Totalling 54,380 personnel in November 1918, it provided food, equipment, motorised transport, trains, boats, donkeys, mules, camels and men.
Again... for a fuller history of the ASC jump to the appendix.

# RETROSPECT

## Other campaigns & the enemy

*"Unlike British Armies in France, we were not a gigantic force; we only dealt in thousands, where France dealt in the millions"* - Badcock

It is easy to forget that the war of 1914-1918 was a World War. Campaigns raged across the globe; besides the battles being fought by the Egyptian Expeditionary Force and the fighting in France, there was fighting in East Africa, Mesopotamia and Salonica, not to mention the War at sea and the battles in the Pacific.

East Africa had many issues with distance and a lack of communication and supplies from home. Salonica (Macedonian Front) began as a British Expeditionary Force action before becoming one of Inter-Allied Forces. Mesopotamia was initially controlled by forces from India.

Abbreviations – used throughout the text.

| | |
|---|---|
| *M.E.F* | *Mediterranean Expeditionary Force* |
| *E.E.F* | *Egyptian Expeditionary Force* |
| *NCO* | *Non Commissioned Officer* |
| *C-in-C* | *Commander-in-Chief* |
| *A.I.F* | *Australian Imperial Force* |
| *G.H.Q* | *General Headquarters* |
| *G.O.C* | *General Officer Commanding* |
| *A.D.C* | *Aide-de-camp* |
| *M.B* | *Medical Board* |
| *A.S.C* | *Army Service Corps* |
| *R.A.S.C.* | *Royal Army Service Corps* |
| *C.S.M.* | *Company Sergeant Major* |
| *ANZAC* | *Australian and New Zealand Army Corps* |
| *Q.M.G* | *Quartermaster General* |
| *K.S.O.B* | *King's Own Scottish Borderers* |
| *P.M.L.O.* | *Principal Military Landing Officer* |
| *IX A.C.* | *(Acting Commander)* |

# ALDERSHOT

When the Kaiser started the 1914-18 War, I was Adjutant of my Corps at Aldershot and there I remained till February 1915. There were not many idle moments during those 5 months! Fortunately something would turn up from time to time to raise a laugh. In the first few weeks of August there was a tremendous rush of men to join up, all volunteers, of course, who received the princely stipend of those days of ½d.

The numbers joining were so great that clothing and equipment and accommodation could not compete, so a halt was called.

When recruiting was reopened, the initial rush had lost its impetus and the Powers-That-Were decided to offer the bait of 6/-a day pay plus a £5 bonus discharge.

That caught on alright, except amongst those who had been the first to join. Presently, amongst the 6/- a day gents, a considerable number developed disturbing symptoms of epilepsy, frothing at the mouth etcetera. Naturally they were discharged and given their £5 bounties.

*One day my RSM thought he recognised one of these discharged epileptics as a new recruit. Yes! He was right and later we found out that this astute gentleman, by using soap in his mouth to produce the requisite froth, had collected over £30 by being discharged from different units!*

*Another money making device was practised by some hastily appointed acting NCOs. Recruits, on enlistment, were given passes for a week or 14 days, so as to ease the problem of accommodation and feeding, but certain of these NCOs used to levy a toll on each pass and as they were handling several hundred a week the cash was rolling in nicely, but that too, was run to ground!*

*A third game was that of blankets. Recruits would arrive at all hours of the twenty four and those who came at night were given a couple of blankets and told to doss down in the Riding School. It wasn't long before some recruits found how easy it was to "collect" a tidy number of blankets and dispose of them for cash in the town of Aldershot. Yes! We scotched that, as well, in the end.*

There was no conscription at the start of the War, it was the time of the volunteer army; the 'Pals'; men eager to sign up to serve their King & Country alongside their friends & family. Conscription was introduced in January 1916 and though it was initially aimed at single men aged 18-41, within a few months, it was rolled out for married men.

It is fair to say that a large proportion of these men were from working class backgrounds and would have been on wages of around 16s 9d a week. The Army would have been a very nice potential earner; after all the War would be 'over by Christmas'. Within the first two months of recruiting around half a million men signed up to serve, a number far exceeding the aim of raising 100,000 troops.

Despite this desire to serve, it is clear that some were after something very different and sought to take advantage of the situation. Estimating for inflation, that £5 bonus discharge would be worth around £530.00 today! The fellow who managed to collect £30.00 (approx. £3180 today) had done rather well for himself!

The other two money making schemes show how opportunists could take advantage of the situation they unexpectedly found themselves in!

This image is a far cry from the idea of the young lads who signed up, the Lions led by Donkeys, a side we are unused to seeing when we think about WW1.

# RETROSPECT

# GALLIPOLI

*Early in February 1915 I found myself at Avonmouth in the Dunlace Castle bound for the lord knows where.*

Once mobilized he did not see England again till 1919 and during the first weeks of mobilization never took off uniform nor did his chief, his Clerk nor the RSM, all had 24 hr days.

*The one bright spot for me being that I was a Ship's Adjutant, which meant I had a cabin to myself, a benediction to anyone like myself, a bad sailor. By mid-March we arrived at that vast semi-inland lake, Mudros Bay and just inside the narrow rocky entrance we had our first view of that famous battleship - Queen Elizabeth.*

The Gallipoli Campaign, the famous amphibious landings that took place between 19 Feb 1915 – 9 Jan 1916 on the Gallipoli Peninsula, Turkey. Thousands of the Mediterranean Expeditionary Force-British, ANZAC and French troops landed on the rocky beaches with the aim of pushing back the Turks and ending the Middle Eastern War at a stroke.

Badcock had arrived at the island of Lemnos, around 31 miles from the Dardanelles and Gallipoli. Moudros or Mudros as it was known to the British, was the town and harbour used as a base for the invasion. It was also the place where the Armistice of Mudros was signed on 30th October 1918, ending the War with the Ottoman Empire. Although the harbour was suitable for naval ships from both the British and French Navies, it had little infrastructure to support an army on land, with the result that many of the troops to be deployed at Gallipoli, underwent training in Egypt.

*We had several hundred horses and mules onboard and the next morning I was one of others to accompany the Base Commandant in a ships rowing boat to the jetty at Mudros East, where we hoped to find a suitable site for a horse depot.*

*A naval pinnace lay by the jetty and, as our General climbed ashore, he espied an Admiral and his staff at the shore-end of the jetty - and the admiral clearly did ditto. I can see him now adjusting his eye glass. Our General saluted and announced that he had come here to find a camp for the horses and mules aboard the Dunlace Castle. In a few well chosen words the Admiral made it plain that he was Governor of Mudros and before any livestock could be landed on the island it would be as well first to get approval.*

*The Admiral's staff, amongst them a small midshipman, clearly knew their chief as a man of action and for a split second it seemed likely our General might have to seek the sanctuary of our ships rowing boat. The Admiral was one Weymss, the General - McGrigor, the Midshipman -*

the General's son and lately - First Sea Lord! I wonder if he remembers this incident of over 40 years ago?

The Admiral Rosslyn Erskine Wemyss, 1st Baron Wester Wemyss, G.C.B., C.M.G., M.V.O. was sent to Mudros ahead of the Gallipoli Campaign to prepare for the landings. He commanded a squadron during the landing of British and French troops at Cape Helles on 25th April 1915. Wemyss also oversaw the re-embarkation of the troops from Suvla & ANZAC Cove in December 1915 following the failure of the campaign. Following successful War Service, Wemyss was the senior British representative at the signing of the Armistice on the 11th November 1918.

The General, Major General Charles Rhoderic Robert McGrigor C.B., C.M.G. and the Midshipman (some sources say he was a Lieutenant at the time) Rhoderick McGrigor, who later became First Sea Lord in 1951.

*Gallipoli! How clear in one's old age those events of 1915 still seem. It is akin to what the immortal Mr John Jorrocks said- "In that word' uniting what a ramification of knowledge is compressed"!*

*To begin, let me record my first sight of the Australian Imperial troops, Maclagan's brigade, returning from a route march to their camp at Mudros. I have never seen a finer body of men physically before or since, they were all endowed with the frame of a Keith Miller, the present day great Australian cricketer. Aye! Wild as hawks, maybe they were, but they were MEN!*

*The Turks and Germans learnt that too, before World War No1 ran to its appointed end.*

# RETROSPECT

Maclagan's Brigade was the 3rd Brigade, AIF and was the first landed at ANZAC Cove. Maclagan was actually a Scotsman who had been seconded to the Australian Army back in 1901 and later went on to command on the Western Front.
   Keith Miller (1919-2004) was an Australian test cricketer and a Royal Australian Air Force pilot during World War II. He is widely regarded as Australia's greatest ever all-rounder.

> *So long as the history of the British Army remains, that great division the XXIX, will never be forgotten by all the Regular battalions of long service men, collected from overseas. When they went ashore at the various beaches collectively known as Helles on 25 April 1915, orders had been given that no man was to use his water bottle without permission from an Officer. The landings were made at 5am, the day was very hot, so was the fighting. A friend of mine later told me how, round about 5pm, this CSM asked if the men might have a drink, the first in 12 ghastly hours. That's discipline if you like.*

Helles or Cape Helles was made up of 5 beaches around the Gallipoli Peninsula – S beach, V beach, W beach, X beach, Y Beach. Each beach has its own story of victory and loss. The landings were ultimately a failure, but the courage of both sides should not be underrated nor understated.
   Amongst Badcock's papers are notes he made whilst at Gallipoli and was landing on W.Beach on the 24th April 1915. The full account can be read in the Appendix, but to summarise, it was not all plain sailing!

Cape Helles W Beach 1915

*Some 3 months later, in August, we made a new landing at Sulva Bay. All the troops were new Army divisions. Our landing was practically unopposed; all men went ashore with 2 full water bottles, and I will hazard a guess that by 9am there were mighty few water bottles which had a drop of water left in them.*

The landings at Suvla Bay were part of the August Offensive between 6th-15th August and the final push by the British & Imperial forces to try and break the stalemate at Gallipoli. Suvla Bay was located further north on the Peninsula, away from the other beach landings but only 5km from ANZAC cove, which became an objective later in the landing. The aim was to link up Suvla & ANZAC and resulted in the battles of Scimitar Hill & Hill 60, on 21st August 1915.

# RETROSPECT

*Having met with little opposition at first, the engagement was again mismanaged and became another nail in the coffin of an already ill-fated campaign.*

Badcock was witness to the events and recorded his experiences, which, though too long to list here in full, speak of miscommunication between Commanders against a background of constant, yet not overly heavy, fire experienced during the landings. He also as you might expect, focuses on the logistical situation, particularly concerning the landing of mules or rather the lack of or the wrong location for mule landings and without the most precious resource of all – water. Here water was not only important for the men but also for the animals which also had to go without water if there was none to hand.

"I explain what help roads would be, but that neither P.M.L.O nor IX A.C. apparently considers it comes within their jurisdiction. 32 carts and 303 mules landed up to 8 p.m. The country up to the firing line consists of tracks suitable for pack transport only; but which could readily and easily be made possible for wheel transport. Water is VERY VERY scarce, our only source of supply being from water-lighters, and none of the mules landed to-day has a drop to drink, though they've been working from the moment they landed." - ***Appendix to War Diary August 1915***

*Were these New Army men to blame? I think not, for they had never been trained as hard as the men who comprised the famous XXIXth.*

The XXIXth or 29th Division embarked at Avonmouth about a month after Badcock had set sail. The Division was one the first to land at Cape Helles on 25th April 1915 with the M.E.F and saw fierce fighting there. Later they moved on to Sulva. Being one of the last units to be evacuated, the Division returned to Egypt before redeploying to France and the Western Front. The Division itself was made up of three Brigades, the 86th, 87th & 88th, as well as several artillery units.

The XXIXth may not be famous today but they do have quite a War record. They took part in the early beach landings of Gallipoli, including the landings at V & W Beaches which met with fierce Turkish resistance. The other three were largely unopposed. They fought in various battles on the Peninsular including the first, second and third battle of Krithia as well as the Battle of Gully Raine. They also saw action following the landings at Suvla in the Battle of Scimitar Hill. Following the evacuation, the Division served on the Somme and suffered heavy losses.

In a series of private letters between Badcock and Brigadier C.E.R. Ince, C.B., C.B.E. in 1965, Badcock remarks about a recent letter in the Telegraph. The letter concerned the lack of any plans to provide water for the troops at Suval in 1915. The fact the Telegraph was printing letter about WW1 in the 1960's seems to go against the publishers denial to print Retrospect some 10 years before.

*"In point of fact- we- (the army-) had made v.careful plans: I was the bloke. Sent over by Koz (DTS. GHQ) to implement it. The plan was 3 ships (Dundrenan, Kentucky & St Oswald) with over a total of 2000 pack mules + filled water carrying receptacles were to be inside the boom at Suvla at dawn the day we landed.*

> *I the Navy - (Captain Roger Keyes C o S to Wemyss - the Admiral) had undertaken to have the ships there- they never appeared till 3 days later! (both 3 and later are underlined 3 times in the letter) by which time the Turks had tumbled to what our 3 New Army Divs had planned to do & saw to it that we did not do it!"* - Badcock Letter

Badcock goes on to say

> "*I wrote a short note to the D.T. telling them the acts, but they have ignored it - or you must never (again underlined three times) criticise The Royal Navy. They can do no wrong!!! Churchill may have been right over Gallipoli strategically but he also "bitched" the show from the start though his impatience to gain renown for the Navy instead of waiting for the army to lend a hand-a guardsman, Stopford was GOC troops at Suvla – he had a bad bout of gout & ran operations from a deck chair on HMS Jonquil (a light cruiser) in Suvla Bay his AQMG was one J.T. Kearns ex Riding Master at Woolwich of our Corps in 1904, when I was there & later City Marshall!! I made several trips out to HMS Jonquil to try and get news of my 3 shiploads of Mules & water –but to no effect.*
>
> "*The 3 divisions landed at Suvla ( the X, XI & XIII were all new army Divs- quite untrained in water discipline, let alone- in fighting- & each and went ashore with 2 filled water bottles & I'd lay a shade of odds there were few with any water left in them by 0900 that day.*"

Badcock then goes on to discuss in the same letter *"fun the Yanks are having in Vietnam.'*

Now, returning to Retrospect

> *I wonder how many folk who many have read of Gallipoli and later Sinai and Palestine, realise what the river Nile in Egypt meant to us in 1915 '16 and '17, for practically all the water we used came from there. In Gallipoli, by steamer to Mudros and Imbros and thence by small craft, familiarly known as Beetles, to the three beaches of Helles, Anzac and Surla. In Palestine, by 12" water pipes from the filter plant at Kantara, fed by the so-called Sweet-water Canal.*

> *I have never ceased to marvel at what filtration can accomplish when I think of that sweet-water canal running from the Nile at Cairo, via Zagazig to Tel-el-Kebir and Ismailia, where it divides, one branch south to Suez, the other, north to Port Said.*

> *It was used for a multiplicity of purpose by the local population living along its banks as well as by their water buffaloes.*

One of the key players behind the supply of water during the campaign was Brigadier-General Everard McLeod Blair of the Royal Engineers. During the War he directed the laying of hundreds of miles of pipeline across the Sinai Desert and then further extending it to Palestine. Blair was recalled to Britain in March 1917, a month before the pipeline was completed, following the second battle of Gaza in April. This water coming all the way from Egypt kept the army alive whilst it slogged away against the Turkish Lines.

*Flies however were surely our greatest curse in Gallipoli. You couldn't put down your knife on a plate without the blade being instantly obliterated by a black mass of these. I doubt if anyone escaped one or more attacks of dysentery during the 6 summer months. Surely these infernal flies must hold the all-time worlds record for reproduction, and they appear indestructible. For the first 48 hours after we went ashore at Suvla in August there wasn't a fly to be seen, and then they came in their millions, from somewhere.*

*Some great soldiers attained immortality by having public houses named after them, but few, I imagine, for having given their names to a latrine seat with a lid! Yet that is what that great polo player of the Durham Light Infantry and one time famous commander of the XXIXth division achieved in Gallipoli a de Lisle! Yes! He did all he could to fight against the flies and dysentery.*

*Readers of Mr Jorrocks will remember his advice to ingenuous youth always to count ten before he viewed a fox away. Sound advice, and not only in the hunting field.*

Mr Jorrocks was a Cockney grocer created by the 19th century cartoonist Robert Smith Surtees. Dating from the 1830's Mr Jorrocks was a great success with the public, his mainstay being anything relating to Fox Hunting.

The Turks and the weather were not the only enemy the Allies faced at Gallipoli. Disease and dysentery were rife with 45 percent loses from diarrhoea in one battalion alone.

*One day a V.I.P from Australia paid a visit to Anzac round about July 1915 when the heat was full on. In conversation with some of his countrymen there he was shocked to learn that they had had no meat ration for several days.*

*He must have departed without asking who was responsible for this apparent failure in supplies, for the first reaction to his discovery which reached us at G.H.Q Imbros, was a peremptory telegram from London, from the Prime Minister, whither V.I.P. had proceeded ex Gallipoli, calling for the immediate execution of the person responsible for starving the A.I.F at Anzac. Fortunately the answer was quite simple. General Birdwood, G.O.C Anzac, had recently asked for a temporary discontinuance of the meat ration during the summer heat and the substitution of tinned fruits. This had been done by purchasing every such tin which could be found in Egypt.*

Who was this V.I.P.? So far research has not revealed his identity, but what this incident highlights is the ease with which miscommunication can occur on the Front Line and how misinterpretation can have dire consequences. Death threats aside, what a feat it must have been to purchase that much tinned fruit and to ship it from Egypt to Gallipoli. Tinned was more important than one at first might think; it was seen by many as a cheap way of preserving food, especially on the Western Front, where soldiers were given low quality food in cans such as the famed 'Bully Beef'.

*A few months after this heat wave, Gallipoli was hit by a blizzard and at Suvla, men were frozen dead in the flooded trenches. Truly a tough land-yet what incredibly beautiful sunsets we used to get with the setting sun lighting up the jagged mountain peaks of Imbros.*

The Island of Imbros, called Gökçeada since 1970, is a Turkish island in the Aegean Sea. During the campaign by the M.E.F it played an important role in supporting the Gallipoli campaign with a hospital, airfield, stores and other administrative support being based there. Like many islands in the Aegean, Imbros had long been a contested Island between Greece and the Ottoman Empire. Following the First Balkan War however, it was one of two Aegean Islands to remain in Ottoman hands, the other being Bozcaada. With the outbreak of War it changed hands again.

*The Navy used to provide daily some form of sea transport to ferry folk from G.H.Q. Imbros over to the beaches and you always got your money's worth at Anzac, for*

*(i) you'd probably have been as sick as the proverbial cat on your trip across,*

*(ii) you knew your ships arrival off Anzac, would be a signal for the Turks at Gaba Tepe to start enfilading the narrow beach where you'd begin the inevitable game of musical chairs, running like a rabbit from one pile of bully beef boxes to the next as each burst of firing ceased; and*

*(iii) at Quinn's Post you could heave a jam tin filled with explosive at the Turkish trenches less than a cricket pitch away, but not between 1 and 2pm. A gentleman's*

*agreement enacted that period was for sleep-for both sides!*

Gaba Tepe or Kabatepe was where an Ottoman artillery battery was positioned during the Gallipoli offensive. Attempts to capture it by ANZAC forces failed and the bombardments continued. It is nice to see that even in the heat of war when the lines are only 22 yards away from one another, both sides understood the need for a midday rest.

*What totally different human beings our two C-in- C in Gallipoli were.*

*Ian Hamilton, who seemed to know only his immediate staff and Charles Munro, who knew everyone. Munro damaged his leg soon after he took over command, but he always sat on a deck chair on the Aragon (then our G.H.Q.) in Mudros Bay, with another chair by his side, and anyone coming aboard would be hailed, told to sit down and questioned. He learnt a great deal that way and the individual thus questioned regarded his C-in-C as a personal friend. What a magnetic effect that can have on an army!*

*Archibald Murray, who succeeded Munro, after we had cleared out of Gallipoli and were back in Egypt, was like Ian Hamilton in that respect. General Allenby, 18 months later Murray's successor, was like Munro, but even more so.*

*"Lions led by donkeys"*, a common phase relating to men and officers of the First World War. The concept was far from a new way of looking at the armed forces and had links back to the Crimean War and Arabic proverbs. There has been much debate over the years as to whether this is an accurate portrayal

of Officers during WW1. What is clear is that the underlying character of Commanders can win or lose a wars as well as the character of those fighting.

Ian Hamilton, had a long military service and lived to the age of 94. He took command of the Gallipoli campaign at the age of 62 and though more experienced than most, faced many difficulties before and during the campaign, mostly not of his own making or out of his control. He was recalled on the 16th October 1915.

Charles Munro took command during the later stages of Gallipoli Campaign and ordered the evacuation following many discussions with the War Office in London and a visit to Gallipoli from Kitchener himself. Munro had overall strategic charge of evacuating approximately 136,000 men, 17,000 horses and 400 guns of the M.E.F from Gallipoli, without the Turks knowing what was going on. Following the withdrawal, Munro commanded for a short time on the Western Front before being deployed to India as Commander-in-Chief and oversaw the Mesopotamian Campaign.

Hand drawn postcard, Christmas at Gallipoli

## FOR SALE
## August 2nd 1915

*For Sale, or to be let, unfurnished with fixtures, excluding M.E.F., fine freehold property, known as "Q" Court.*

*In the favourite residential Seaside Resort of ANZAC COVE, a charming bungalow 7 feet above the sea, standing in its own fenced ground, 1/360th of an acre, approached by a pretty winding road, comprising one large double bedroom and old oak lounge hall, with westerly aspect and superb sea view.*

*Telephone installed in all rooms, outdoor sanitation, Incinerator practically on the property. Grand old timber, removed en bloc from the Château de Lotbinière (during the absence of the owner).*

*Within 30 seconds of the Beach and overlooking Pier, 2 seconds to the local post office, but 2 months between deliveries.*

*Equidistant from Messrs. Marsh and Worsley, General Providers; nearest church, St. Mary's, Alexandria, 4 day excluding delays at MUDROS. Sea bathing (un-mixed) Beach full of interest to Conchologists, good rough shooting, big game and coarse fishing go with the property.*

*Daily Trips to HELLES, IMBROS, MUDROS and the Islands of the Aegean Sea a speciality, arranged by Messrs. Lesslie & Co., (who do not guarantee date of return) the sea being frequently either too rough or too smooth.)*

*Rent, at a war sacrifice, on application to Messrs Bola Singh, Littler & Co., Sanitary Experts, who have inspected and recommended the property. Available on next Ides of March or on capture of Achi Ba.*

For Sale, a loose page from Badcock's archive typed on official headed paper and the date scribbled in pencil, dropped in just behind his accounts of his time at Helles, Gallipoli.

Once you put it into context it shows that even in the desperate times of War, there is humour to be found, despite the blazing heat and mind numbing cold accompanied by the sound of exploding shells filling the air whilst bullets whizz past!

To protect themselves from the shrapnel and bullets, soldiers had a range of headwear available to them, although it wasn't until September 1915 that the iconic Brodie helmet was introduced and even then, only a very limited supply was issued.

Hand drawn postcard, Christmas at Gallipoli

The soldiers at Gallipoli, in common with those on the Western Front, had to rely upon a range of other headwear to keep them safe… the British Winter forage cap (Gor Blimey winter cap), the regular Stiff cap, Worsley and foreign service Pith helmets, Slouch hats, Balaclavas, the Glengarry, Pattern 1905 'Stiff' cap, Gurhka slouch hat and Turban headdress for Indian Troops to name a few.

The navy of course had their own varieties, most common was the sailors cap, which many will have seen being worn by Donald Duck. Though these might keep soldiers warm, they were a poor defence against snipers and shrapnel. The Brodie itself was not designed to stop a direct hit, more to help deflect the deadly metal flying through the air.

In fact, in the Motorised Transport Units, slouched hats were used in lieu of sun-helmets. The helmets bumped against the back of the drivers seats and had the habit of falling over the eyes whilst the vans bumped along the roads.

Achi Baba was a strategic objective of the Gallipoli offensive as it was the main position of the Ottoman defences. Despite four attempts to capture the heights, it remained out of the Allies hands for the duration of the Campaign. Attempts to capture Achi Baba led to a situation similar to that of the Western Front with prolonged trench warfare.

Château de Lotbinière probably refers to Engineer Col. Joly de Lotbiniere who built eight floating piers in Alexandria designed to bring fresh water to Gallipoli. Originally the Navy was due to tow these into position, however they gave the job over to a private contractor who cut them loose and they sank.

# RETROSPECT

# EGYPT

Egypt the ancient land of the Pharaohs and of the British from 1882 until 1956 and the Suez Crisis. British rule in Egypt has been classified into three distinct phases; Veiled Protectorate- 1882-1913, Formal Protectorate - 1914-1922 & Continued Occupation -1922-1956. Before the outbreak of WW1, Egypt was formally part of the Ottoman Empire.

The British had a considerable amount of control and, although the Sultan was Head of State, real power lay with the British Consul-General, largely because of British control of the Suez Canal. Britain was given the task of protecting the canal following the Convention of Constantinople in 1888 but had effectively assumed control in 1882.

The canal has been called the jugular of the British Empire and, at the time, it was. It was the Gateway to India and the British Empire in the East. Control had to be maintained.

At the outbreak of War, the British declared a formal Protectorate over Egypt deposing the Khedive (the Viceroy of Egypt under the Ottomans-1867-1914) and replacing him with a ruler of their choice. This move ensured that Britain now had full control of the country and could tighten its grip on the Canal, which was attacked more than once by Turkish Troops early in the war.

An attempt to take the Suez Canal took place between 26th January - 4th February 1915 with Ottoman forces under German Command.

The attack failed and the Turks retreated back across the Sinai desert. Surveillance by Allied aircraft removed the possibility of a surprise attack despite Turkish attempts to use diversionary tactics. The strong defence provided by the Indian troops guarding the Canal, ensured the attack would not succeed.

The last ground attack on the Suez Canal came near the Egyptian town of Romani between 3rd & 5th August 1916, when British & Imperial troops again defeated a combined attack from German and Turkish Forces.

This was the end of the land based threat on the Canal ensuring that shipping could flow and saw the start of the Sinai and Palestine campaign.

Control of Egypt meant that there was now a staging post for the Gallipoli, Sinai and Palestine campaigns where the ANZAC and other Imperial troops could be based and trained before being deployed. It also offered a relatively safe place for those injured to recover and have some much needed R&R.

Following the retreat from Gallipoli, the remains of the M.E.F returned to Egypt which resulted in there being three separate military commands in the Country- the M.E.F., the Forces already in Egypt and a separate base at the Levant which held stores for military operations in the region. Which led to all sorts of issues.

In March 1916 there was a reorganisation and the M.E.F. and Forces in Egypt merged to form the Egyptian Expeditionary Force.

A prayer recorded in Badcocks personal papers summarises the three military commands in Egypt. Sadly the second page has been cut in half and one half is missing.

## AFTER MORNING PARADE
## QUICUNQUE VULT

WHOSOEVER will be decorated: before all things it is necessary that he hold the Mediterranean Faith.

Which faith except everyone do keep whole and undefiled; without doubt he shall be stellenbosched everlastingly.

And the Mediterranean Faith is this: that we worship one G.O.C. in Trinity in Unity.

Both confounding the Generals and damming their commands.

For there is one General of Egypt, another of the M.E.F. and another of the Levant Base.

But the Authority of Egypt, of the M.E.F. and of the Levant Base is all one, the Glory equal, the Majesty co-eternal.

Such as Egypt is, such is the M.E.F., and such is the Levant Base.

Egypt separate, the M.E.F. separate, and the Levant Base separate

Egypt incomprehensible, the M.E.F. incomprehensible, and the Levant Base incomprehensible.

Egypt futile, and the M.E.F. futile, and the Levant Base futile. And yet there are not three futiles, but one futiles.

As also there are not three incomprehensible, nor three separates, but one inchoate and one incomprehensible.

So likewise Egypt is Almighty, the M.E.F. is Almighty, and the Levant Base is Almighty.

And yet there are not three almighties, but one almighty.

So Maxwell is G.O.C., Murray is G.O.C. and Altham is G.O.C.

And yet there cannot be three G.O.C.'s but one G.O.C.

So likewise Maxwell is boss, Murray is boss and Altham is boss;

For like as we are compelled by the Army Regulations to acknowledge every General by himself to be G.O.C. and boss;

So we are forbidden by the Lord Kitchener; to say there be three G.O.C.'s or three bosses.

Egypt is made on none; both separate and misbegotten.

Returning to Retrospect

*G.H.Q. in Cairo was located in a vast hotel and one day Murray sent an ADC for my Chief to see him, as he was away inspecting I had to fit the bill. I entered the presence and in reply to his questions told him who I was and what my work was.*

*The C in C strode across the room, stood on two chairs, a leg on each, on a highly polished floor, reached up towards a huge map of Sinai and Palestine and pointing with a pencil asked me if we had sufficient transport to meet the needs of "X" division for an advance from the line Gaza-Beersheba, northwards, to Jaffa-Jerusalem. Before I could give any reply the two chairs decided to skid rapidly apart and I made a perfect rugby tackle by catching the C in C in my arms. After that, there was no further trouble.*

General Sir Archibald James Murray GCB, GCMG, CVO, DSO, had a track record of looking at large maps in a different way.

Following the invasion of France by the German Empire, he was found with a set of large maps of the invasion spread out on the floor of his hotel room, on all fours, dressed only in his underwear, while the chambermaids came and went. One would hope at least as a British Officer they were clean.

Following his service on the Western Front, Murray was given command of British Forces in Egypt in January 1916. Egypt was the base of operations responsible for both the Gallipoli & Macedonian Fronts. Murray was also responsible for granting permission for T.E Lawrence to undertake his work with the Arabs and was later relieved by the man known as 'The Bull', Lord Allenby.

*I cannot imagine a man more fitted to command an army than Lord Allenby. He inspired confidence. He never courted popularity. He was a great disciplinarian, but was very just and very human and what a magnificent job he did in Palestine and Syria in 1917 and 1918. He started his innings as our C in C on 28th June 1917, having reached Cairo by train late one evening and by noon next day he had been round every office at GHQ spending a few minutes at each and asking straightforward questions to which he expected similar answers.*

*On a later occasion he had an amusing encounter with a trooper in an Australian Light Horse Regiment uniform, who he noticed wearing South African medal ribbons.*

> *"Well" he asked "are we going to give the Turks a good hiding?" Came the answer slick and to the point; "I'm B-g-d. If I know. That your b-y business"!*

At the time, many people considered that the British Army was ill prepared for WW1, for both men and equipment. It is easy to forget that not that long before, the British, Australian and New Zealand troops had been fighting the Second Boer War (1899-1902), a War for which, at its outbreak they were also considered to be overconfident and ill-prepared.

Many of the British Commanders who led in WW1 served in some way during the Boer War including Lord Kitchener, Allenby and Haig. Many others in this account also cut their military teeth there.

The Boer War was a different kind of war, having fewer pitched battles and more guerrilla warfare, a very stark difference to the trenches of northern Europe and the Deserts of the Middle East.

The experience gained in fighting that war, had an impact on the skills and tactics used by the Commanders in this new War. Allenby himself came from a Cavalry background, a background he put to good use with his use of cavalry and mounted troops whilst fighting the Turks.

The Bull took command on the 27th June, 1917. More than just a change of Commander, his appointment was a change in the British mind-set; maybe, just maybe, the War would not be won only on the Western Front where things had ground to a halt. Allenby was ordered to move at speed. This front has become more than a side show though many still thought it to be a picnic.

When Allenby was first told of his new Command he thought it was a joke!

He was not the first choice of Commander. Jan Smuts, the South African General had been offered the appointment but refused because of his view that the War Office had little enthusiasm for the Near East Theatre of War. Prior to taking up his new posting, Allenby had been serving on the Western Front where he commanded the Cavalry Division at Mons and the first battle of Ypres, also leading the V Corps at the second battle of Ypres.

Allenby is often associated with anger and bullish temper, hence his nickname The Bull. On the 31st July 1917 he was informed of the death of his Son on the Western Front.

He broke down in tears in public, reciting a poem by Rupert Brookes. Far from being seen as a sign of weakness, this display of emotion endeared him to his men and officers. The fact that he also got on with the job in hand, made them respect him even more.

Amongst Badcock's personal collection of papers, is a photograph of an as yet, unidentified woman with a stick in hand. A man who seems to be in uniform, is just out of focus on the right hand side.

The location is unknown, but given the sand dune in the background, it is easy to imagine that the photo was taken somewhere in Egypt or Palestine. No matter the subject of the photograph or where it was taken, the image brings to mind a story about Lady Allenby which was recounted by historian Cyril Falls after hearing it at a dinner in London from Allenby himself.

Lady Allenby went out to Cairo shortly after the death of her son Michael which as already mentioned, had a great affect on Allenby. Lady Allenby was given permission by the War Office to travel to see her husband, it did not refuse a C-in-C.

Allenby had taken his Wife up to an observation post within easy range of the Turkish Artillery. 'It was a hot day and the first thing she did was to put up a white parasol', then with a slight smile he added in his gruff voice: 'I soon had that taken down'.

It is easy to imagine a British Lady, dressed in white, standing in a dusty desert observation post with the C-in-C. Being a hot day, she would naturally to put up a cooling white parasol, without even thinking that it would be an open invitation to the Turkish gunners, who if they were watching, could have bought a much swifter end to the war.

After the War Allenby continued his work in the Middle East, appointed High Commissioner for Egypt and Sudan until he retired from active service in 1925. The post war years were not as peaceful as one might have hoped. Egypt was a constant powder keg ready to explode. Allenby even struggled to find any Egyptian willing to head a Government, the threat of assassination being all too real.

Could this be Lady Allenby? (Unknown woman in desert)

A photo of an unknown officer not from the events described above but still rather fun. On the back it reads "some lightrefreshment before going after pig."

# RETROSPECT

# PALESTINE

*G.H.Q. did not remain long in Cairo after Allenby's arrival and we soon located in the desert some miles south of Gaza, but prior to our move there I had attended a conference at General Chetwode's headquarters at Deir el Belah.*

*The conference was run by Guy Dawnay; he drew a rough map of Palestine and Syria- put in our dispositions and those of the Turks, along the then front, Gaza-Beersheba. He explained the plan of attack, the follow up to the line Jaffa-Jerusalem, after that, to Beirut-Damascus and finally Alexandretta-Aleppo.*

G.H.Q. had been based at the Savoy Hotel but was moved to a camp at Um el Kelab which was near the city of Rafa. In stark contrast to the comfort and luxury of the Savoy this new desert command centre was hot and fly ridden, but most importantly it allowed Allenby direct contact with his troops.

Deir el Belah is a city that is today in the central Gaza Strip about 16 Km from the Egyptian border and 20 Km south of West Gaza. It was captured by British forces following the

Surf Boat- Deir el Belah

surrender of Khan Yunis, another city in the region on the 28th February 1917. It's capture was of strategic importance as it forced the Turkish forces to pull out back towards Gaza and Beersheba.

The British were also able to establish a railhead by April 1917 and shortly afterwards an aerodrome was set up along with the camp at Um el Kelab. An extract from a letter from Chetwode (10/3/17) also identifies the area as having ample water but not many drinking wells and roads in the area being in bad shape.

> *He then pushed his spectacles back on his forehead, struck a match, burnt his map, smiled saying 'I haven't mentioned a word of this yet to the Baronet" (Gen Chetwode).*
>
> *Well! 15 months later, by the end of October 1918, that is, every item in this plan of Guy Dawnay had been accomplished, though he himself did not see it through*

*in its entirety, as he left us, together with another great soldier, Sir Herbert Lawrence, to serve on Lord Haig's staff in France.*

*It had been my good fortune to have had much to do with Guy Dawnay since Gallipoli days.*

*He had a remarkable brain coupled with a wonderful vision – and he was a guardsman. He sowed the seed in 1917 which Allenby brought to fruition later that year and in 1918, with his supreme handling of events.*

Guy Dawnay was a Coldstream Guards Officer who served both in the Palestine campaign and on the Western Front, under General Haig.

In the Seven Pillars of Wisdom T.E. Lawrence described Dawnay as "mainly intellect. He was cold, shy minded but always thinking,"

Lawrence goes on to say "Beneath this mathematical surface he hid passionate many-sided convictions, a reasoned scholarship in higher warfare and the brilliant bitterness of a judgement disappointed with us, and with life.

He was the least professional of soldiers, a banker who read Greek history, a strategist unashamed".

Dawnay was involved in the planning of the attack at Suvla and the battle of Gaza and it is interesting to reflect on the different man that Lawrence and Badcock seem to describe.

Badcock is likely to have had more day to day dealings with Dawnay particularly because of his involvement at Gallipoli. What they do seem to agree on is his ability to strategize and plan, after all in 1918, the British defeated the Turks.

Not everyone agrees with these observations. In letters between Badcock and the historian Cyril Falls dating from

1964 about his book "Armageddon 1918", Falls disputes the idea that "Guy Dawnay could have been the brains behind ALL the Commander in Chief's plans or in fact of that with which I was most concerned because he had gone to G.H.Q. in France and been succeeded by my lamented friend Bart Bartholomew who certainly put the details into Allenby's plans but did not conceive them. In fact as I have written, it was a venture which could have been conceived only by the Commander in Chief."

In reply to this letter Badcock sent Falls a collection of Dawnay's notes that alas are lost to time. Although these notes failed to change Falls mind, Falls goes on to mention that he met Dawnay once at a dinner party held by the author and playwright Edward Plunkett but does not elaborate further. Like many events of the past the whole truth can never be fully known which is one thing that makes it all the more exciting!

> *One September 1917 afternoon I was having a cup of tea at General Chetwode's headquarters in the desert at a spot called El Fukhari.*
>
> *His Mess hut was a "rush" one with fly-proof netting and the floor was dug some feet below the sand level to give additional headroom- the mess table was covered with a spotlessly clean tablecloth and a vase with red pomegranate flowers rested on top.*
>
> *I couldn't refrain from saying how wonderfully pleasant it was to find such a haven in the desert, where the corps commander remarked, "it is a great mistake not to make yourself as reasonably comfortable as you can just because you are on active service.*
>
> *Look at Charles Dobell" he went on, "he came up to fight the battle of Gaza and I offered him a tent etc etc,*

*but No, he didn't want any tent, so he lay out in the sun with a map spread out in front of him, kept down by stones, and a field-telephone glued to his ear. Well! He got sunstroke, a damned good hiding, and a blower-hat, and deserved all three."!*

El Fukhari or Fukhari is located in Southern Palestine (modern day Israel) and close to where the Battle of Buqqar Ridge took place on the 27th October 1917, towards the end of the stalemate following the Second Battle of Gaza.

Charles Dobell, fought in the Kamerun Campaign during WW1, a campaign intended to capture German Colonies in what is today the Republic of Cameroon and parts of Gabon, Congo, Central African Republic, Chad and Nigeria.

He was then redeployed to the E.E.F following a knighthood and is considered largely responsible for the two failed attempts to capture Gaza, a task he was personally given by Murray. Although not entirely his fault, he was relieved of command and sent to India in disgrace.

The First Battle of Gaza took place south of Gaza following the British push to recapture the Sinai Peninsula in January 1917. The First Battle took place in March 1917 and saw the British try to penetrate deep into Palestine, but were pushed back with victory being on a knife edge.

The Second Battle of Gaza took place in April. After the first Battle, the Ottomans reinforced the Gaza line, resulting in much higher casualties on the second engagement and a Front that developed into trench warfare similar to that of the Western Front, although both sides had open flanks, something both sides were very much aware of! The fortifications meant that a direct assault on the City was effectively ruled out, even when British troop numbers were increased.

The Third Battle of Gaza took place much later, in November 1917. Following the British victory at Beersheba, the E.E.F., now under the command of General Allenby was successful in taking the City, allowing British forces to push back the Turks and pave the way for the eventual capture of Jerusalem.

The Third Battle of Gaza and capture of Beersheba were all part of a new strategy that was devised by Chetwode. When Allenby took command he reviewed and approved the plans and following an increase in troop numbers they were put into action.

> *General Chetwode was another very great solider, but like all great men he had his likes and dislikes, one of the latter being his inability to understand anyone wearing a shirt without a collar attached! A friend of mine, a Major General, on Chetwodes staff, learnt of this idiosyncrasy when he was late one morning for breakfast and apologising said he had lost his back collar stud "Good God" said the Baronet "you surely don't wear a shirt with a separate collar.*

General Philip Chetwode began WW1 on the Western Front and took part in the First Battle on Ypres in October 1914. Later he was transferred from the War in Europe that had become literally stuck in the mud, to the Middle Eastern Front and given command of the Desert Mounted Corps and saw action in the First Battle of Gaza in March 1917. Following Allenby's appointment he was promoted to command the XX Corps in June 1917 (The Corps first saw action at the battle of Beersheba).

Shirts? Today we take it for granted that the collar of our shirts is attached, as are the cuffs, but of course, it has not always been that way and like all fashion trends, things have changed over time. Fashion choices can reveal a lot about a person, both in character and in wealth.

The first button down shirt as we know today was registered in 1871 but it seems that it wasn't until the 1930's that the shirt we know today became the mainstay!

For Officers it was of course very important to look the part and in a modern army for them to have the most up to date equipment; this goes right down to the shirt on their backs! It also seems very British to take issue with a missing collar in the middle of a war zone in the desert.

> *Lord Allenby, too, held strong views on certain things. He cordially disproved of anyone smoking in the vicinity of an Ammunition Dump; he went off the deep-end if he saw anyone tethering his horse to an olive tree, or riding in shorts. I once heard him address a gunner subaltern whom he found smoking perched on some ammunition boxes stacked in the dry sandstone bank of the wadi Ghazze. If that gunner subaltern is still alive, I bet he still remembers the episode!*

One can imagine why the C-in-C might object to men smoking near the ammunition boxes, which at the time were most likely made of wood and very dry. This outburst certainly matches the perceived character of Allenby.

His nature aside, there is another practical reason why smoking near an important resource would give rise to an explosion from the Chief.

Resources were limited for the E.E.F. which was still regarded as playing a part in a sideshow. The Force had to ship in valuable resources and then transport them long distances across inhospitable terrain.

To lose anything, especially to a careless Subaltern (an Officer below the rank of Captain and who should know better) would just not do.

The Wadi Gazzee (also spelt Wadi Gaza) - lies halfway between Gaza and Belah and was, and still is, a formidable obstacle with step sides and a stone bed. Importantly it has access to water, something that is to this day, important in desert warfare, even more so at the time because of the need to water the horses. The Wadi held strategic important for all the Battles of Gaza.

Today there are mixed views on riding in shorts, certainly never to be done in competition. Most of the reasons why shorts should not be worn whilst on horseback, come down to safety and comfort, from legs trapped in the stirrup leather to rubbing on the side of the horse causing sores.

Allenby of course was a Cavalry man before becoming C-in-C. He had served as Inspector General of Cavalry 1910-14 and would expect his men to strictly follow procedure. So in the heat of the desert it is quite understandable that some of the Cavalry would risk the fury of an Officer and wear shorts like their comrades in the Infantry.

Uniform is a major part of any regimented force; we may all recognise the olive greens of the Western Front, but those serving throughout China, Mesopotamia, Palestine and Italy all wore Khaki drill service dress, a sand coloured uniform similar in colour to the one worn by troops today deployed to desert environments. Originally made up of jacket and trousers, shorts quickly became part of the uniform. As was shirtsleeve order where the jacket was removed and sleeves rolled up in an attempt to combat the intense heat!

Other changes included the issuing of pantaloons instead of trousers, canvas leggings instead of puttees and a combined waterproof coat that could also be used as a ground sheet.

There was also another threat that the troops faced- Mosquitos. In fact- nearly 5,000,000 yards of mosquito nets for use of troops in Egypt, Mesopotamia, and Salonika was ordered by the Government from Nottingham and Somersetshire lace manufacturers- Colac Reformer (Victoria) 16th December 1916.

*But the yarn I like best about Lord Allenby is the one which General Bulfin, who was G.O.C of our XXI Corps, used to relate in after years, in his rich Irish brogue. It ran thus. Before the War, one Monsieur Picot had been the French High Commissioner in Syria, but when War broke out he departed for France, leaving, in his hurry, a list of prominent Syrians of Beirut with whom he had been planning a revolt against the Turks.*

*Unfortunately for the prominent Syrians, the Turks got hold of M. Picot's list of starters and Jockeys and duly celebrated their find by stringing up the leading Syrians to the nearest trees! Then, in due course we captured Beirut and Damascus in Oct 1918 and one of the first to return to Syria was none other than M. Picot. It seems he did not regard Lord Allendy's success with the fervour one would have expected,*

*And as there were no longer any Turks for him to play ball with he decided to try his wiles, indirectly, on Lord Allenby, who was soon to learn that the French Government had expressed concern over a report that had reached them that Lord Allenby had been accepting bribes, in the shape of Arab Mares, from King Faisal. As a matter of routine our Government passed this report on to Lord Allenby who promptly made a signal to General Bulfin at his Corps HQs in Beirut saying he would be arriving-giving time and date at his HQ's and that he*

> wished to see Monsieur Picot, as soon as he arrived.
> "Came the day" went on General Bulfin, "and when the chief arrived I could gauge the temperature as I ushered M. Picot into the room and made myself scarce."
> "Have you ever heard the lions fed in the Zoological Gardens"? "Well! It was a noise like that, only more so" continued Gen. Bulfin- "I never heard anything like it! Presently the representative of the French Republic emerged, his collar all pulp, perspiration running down his face and neck, looking like a Jackdaw of Rheims. He will never again" ended Gen Bulfin "be so foolish as to accuse the chief of accepting bribes from King Faisal or anyone else."

To accuse anyone in a time of war or peace of taking bribes is a major accusation, especially if the one you are accusing is the C-in-C of an Army.

Monsieur Francois George Picot, a French diplomat along with the British diplomat Sir Mark Sykes were the architects behind the secret Sykes-Picot agreement, signed 16th May 1916, which effectively divided the Ottoman Empire between the British, French & Russians and led the way for the post-war Mandates.

It was first made public by the Russians following the Russian Revolution and in British newspapers in November 1917. To the embarrassment of many it showed that the British were neglecting their promise to the Arabs who were fighting alongside them for a new homeland.

This accusation does not however seem to be the first time that Allenby and Picot crossed swords!

Following the capture of Jerusalem in December 1917, a celebratory dinner was held by Allenby. Picot was one of the Guests! Over dinner he tried to assert his and the French position that he would take over the Government of Jerusalem. Also on the Guest list was one T.E. Lawrence, (yes the famous Lawrence of Arabia) who later recounted how Allenby very carefully considered his response whilst those around him were eating a 'salad, chicken mayonnaise and foie gras. Sandwiches hung in our wet mouths unmunched'.

They waited and watched to see what the Chief would do. 'His face grew red: he swallowed, his chin coming forward… whilst he said grimly "In the military zone the only authority is that of the Commander-in-Chief - myself"' Picot of course protested this, stating that he and France had been promised a Civil Government. Allenby replied "Sir Edward Grey referred to the Civil French Government which will be established when I judge that the military situation permits".

Sir Edward Grey was a Liberal statesman and British Foreign Secretary who signed the Sykes-Picot Agreement. He is best remembered for saying 'The lamps are going out all over Europe, we shall not see them lit again in our life-time'. Post-war, Picot was appointed High Commissioner of Palestine and Syria. Though the incident may have shocked and alarmed him, he still continued to meddle in regional affairs.

Due to some similarities between the aforementioned events, is it possible that they both are different versions of the same event?

Unlikely given the dates and locations. The later Dinner in Jerusalem seems to make it more likely that the second shouting match took place, further reinforcing the dislike and mistrust between the two men.

In the wider context it is also known that the British were very much opposed to the idea of a Civil Government and the token force of 3000 French troops.

One thing is for sure, there was no love lost between Allenby and Picot.

Then, soon after the Turks had surrendered, there was the incident in which men of the ANZAC mounted Division (General Chaytor) were involved.

The division was encamped near us, at G.H.Q. at Bir Salem and they had been having trouble through thefts at night by Arabs from a nearby Village.

One night, an Australian trooper, chasing an Arab who had pinched his greatcoat from under the fly of the tent, was shot, and killed. As soon as it was light, his mates went to the village and gave the Sheikh till 2pm to hand the men, who had shot their comrade, over- warning the Sheikh that if the men were not handed over by the time appointed, his village would be burnt down. And it was! It burnt for two days. But before being set alight all women and children were removed to a place of safety. The Perimeter of the village was soaked with petrol and paraffin. The Arab casualties were heavy. Whilst all this was taking place, Lord Allenby was miles away to the north (a comparable distance being London to Aberdeen - (546 miles approx) having a look at the railway through the Taurus Tunnel and though a report was sent him at once it took him a day or two to return in his car along those miles of dreadful roads.

As soon as he was back, he ordered a parade of the Division, and then, drawn up on three sides of a square, he addressed them. He recounted their history in the War and the great part they had played, and then he told them exactly what he thought of them for the cold blooded murders which some of them had perpetrated whilst he was away. When he finished the Divisional Commander was in tears.

*Later I was told that the division, who had a pretty shrewd idea of what was coming to them, had decided to 'count him out and not give the Chief a hearing, but I was also told by the C-in-C's chief clerk, who was present making a short hand report of what the chief said, that there wasn't*

*A sound and you could have heard a pin drop in the sand. The Anzac Mounted Division was the last to be sent back to their homeland.*

The events described above have become known as the Surafend affair or Surafend Massacre and is a black mark on the previously unblemished ANZAC military record.

The events took place on 10th December 1918, shortly after the War ended in what is modern day Israel. Without going into too much detail, the events are as described above. The man shot dead was Trooper Leslie Lowry.

There are many accounts of the affair including reports, soldiers tales and official histories, not surprising given that an estimated 200 men took part. HS Gullett, in his book the "A.I.F. in Sinai and Palestine" takes great pains to mention that the people of the region were 'petty' and known for thieving and that they often blamed 'a soldier in a big hat' if a sheep went missing. This background is important to understand the situation and how each side viewed each other.

It is estimated that over 40 people died in the burning which has been traditionally associated with troops from New Zealand. The evidence suggests however that more Australian and British troops were involved than previously thought. Just who was actually involved still remains a bone of contention.

There are various letters and reports on public record saying many different things and Australia still seeks to clear the name of their troops of any wrongdoing, rendering void the disparaging comments Allenby made by calling them cowards and murderers. Allenby's reaction can certainly be seen to be in character.

The Bull was a strong man who held strong views. The official history states that this was an abusive outburst, which can be understood. The ANZAC and Australian Light horse in particular had shown great courage during the War and were held in high regard. Why then would they commit such an atrocity?

What made the situation worse and caused unease, was that Allenby was silent towards the Division for over a year, making them feel as though they had been left out in the cold. It wasn't until a reporter told him of this ill feeling, that Allenby, who was in control of Egypt by now, wrote a glowing report of the actions and his admiration for the Light Horse.

No individuals or divisions were charged with the massacre but compensation was paid in 1921. The Australians paid £515, New Zealand £858 and the British £686, these sums were paid to the British as they had overall charge of Palestine under the mandate of the time.

Could the massacre have been prevented? It does seem so. Reports suggest that Officers on the ground asked for assistance and for police and other troops to intervene. If help had been forthcoming, the outcome could have been very different.

Remember that during WW1 some 20,000 Light Horsemen were deployed. The events at Surafend involved only a handful. As the Australian author and journalist Paul Daley points out - "This incident highlights war's moral complexity and how otherwise good men can do terrible things"

*At his final conference, before the September 1918 operations, with his corps commanders (General Chetwode, Bulfin and Chauvel) Lord Allenby told General Chavvel, who commanded the Desert Mounted Corps, that he was going to issue an order that no great coats were to be carried on the horses so as not impede mobility. The variation between day and night temperatures at this time of the year were very great and General Chauvel remarked that he did not think the order would be a very popular one.*

*Temperatures often went over 35 C and then fell to below freezing at night.*

*"You don't suppose I issue an order for the sake of popularity"? thundered the Chief.*

*"No Sir, I didn't mean that for a moment" replied Chavrel, and then only to land deeper into the mire, "what I meant was it might be a difficult order to get carried out"!*

*"If I give an order I'll see it is carried out all right" was the Chiefs final word.*

*General Chauvel was a most courteous little man. He never failed to send a word of thanks for any small service you may have had the opportunity of doing for him. He handled with marked success subordinate commanders with very strong personalities from his home Dominion – Australia.*

*I remember one such, a very gallant fire eater, affectionately known throughout the E.E.F as "Dame-all-Cox" He commanded the 1st Australian Light Horse Brigade.*

General Chauvel or Sir Harry Chauvel was an Australian Commander who served in the AIF and saw action at Gallipoli & the Sinai and Palestine campaign. He first took command of the 1st Light Horse Brigade (15th August 1914- 6 November 1915) then the ANZAC mounted Division which saw action at the battles of Romani, Magdhaba and of course Gaza.

He was appointed to command the Desert Column/Desert Mounted Corps and became the first Australian to command a Corps leading them through many successful battles including the mounted infantry bayonet charge of Beersheba.

Despite the unfortunate shadow cast on the Light Horse, it was still considered to be such a very strong Brigade. General Charles Cox began his War commanding the 6th Light Horse, serving at Gallipoli before being wounded. When he returned to duty he took permanent command of the 1st Light Horse Brigade in December 1915.

His nickname was 'Fighting Charles' because of his style of command, not a style of command everyone agreed with.

One of the Brigade's most famous moments was at the Battle of Beersheba. Around 500 men and horses charged the Turkish trenches armed only with rifles and bayonets. The action, often referred to as "the last of history's great cavalry charges" was a major success!

Beersheba, a desert city in southern Israel; the Battle for it became part of the Third Battle of Gaza and allowed the British Imperial forces to break the Turkish lines and push on to Palestine. It was also vital that the British capture it quickly due to the lack of water in the area.

Fans of Mel Gibson will also remember that in the film Gallipoli, it is the Light Horse in which he ultimately serves.

Which, on one occasion, was holding a part of our line in the Jordan Valley-North of Jericho. In the small hours of the morning the Brigade Commander was aroused from sleep by his Brigade Major who reported a breakthrough by the Turks in a part of their line- "Kick the b - s out" was all he said and turned over to go to sleep again. Later in the day he sent an equally laconic report to divisional headquarters.

"At 0300 hours this morning the enemy made a slight incursion into my front. I gave immediate orders for the front to be restored. This was done".

Cox held very definite views that it was the duty of a Cavalry Brigade Commander to lead his brigade into battle - whether fighting a mounted or dismounted action, a view not shared by his equally gallant Brigade Major. I can still see that very spectacular mounted attack by Australian Light Horse charging over deep trenches just east of Beersheba on 31 October 1917 which completed the defeat of the Turks at that historic spot.

Later that evening in Beersheba I met an Officer of our G.H.Q. Intelligence Branch. He wore a harassed look. "I've a crowd of Arab Sheiks with me" he explained "and I have been trying to impress them with the might of the British Army. I've shown them 60 par guns- caterpillar-tractors etc. but all that has left them cold."

Little dreaming that it would be of any help to him, I suggested his Sheiks might be interested in a camel convoy now about due to be nearing Beersheba. "There are 20,000 of them, carrying water in fanatic? "I told him.

> *I did not give any more thought to this unit I met the aforesaid officer- (One E.R. Wilson that great slow right hand bowler of 50 years ago for Cambridge and Yorkshire and for years a most popular master at Winchester) some days later, when he greeted me with a smile of thanks, saying, that the gigantic camel convoy (and, at two abreast, it did cover some miles!) just about finished those Arab Sheiks, for they saw something they understood in terms of wealth and power.*

Camels were a vital part of the E.E.F Transport in areas where the soft desert sands were not suitable for mechanical transport – cars, trucks etc., yet it wasn't until December 1915 that the Camel Corps was created. Until then camels had simply been hired, a method that harked back to the earlier days of transport in War.

The creation of the Camel Corps was a great step forward especially considering the Army was regularly dealing with 40,000 camels and their drivers, not to mention scores of donkey teams & horses with their handlers, together with mechanical transport! The subject of motorised transport during the War is a whole series of books within itself. So for now let it suffice that Ford motor vehicles did all the dirty jobs and survived countless breakdowns across inhospitable landscapes.

Many in the west often joked about the value of a Camel, comparing it to the family cow. Take Jack and the Beanstalk for example, in which the family cow was the only thing worth selling. The cow still remains a symbol of wealth in many modern African Tribes.

To many Arabs, camels were not only a source of transport but of food and milk, and as such linked to wealth.

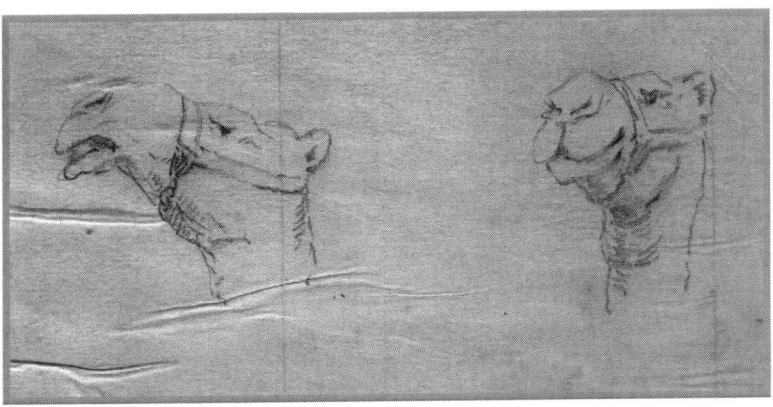

Camel Sketches

Films and popular culture tell us that the value of someone can be valued in camels, a Brides Dowry can be paid with camels and amongst the Bedouin this was certainly true. The Arab Nations had little interest in the might of the British Empire and failed to understand the need for big guns and tractors. What they did know about however, was Camels; in that respect the British were the richest people around.

Simply being supply and pack animals did not mean that the camels and donkeys were safely out of the firing line. They too would often come under attack, yet many proved unconcerned by shell fire and their drivers stood their ground on many occasions, despite the difficult circumstances. The same was also true for many of the donkeys.

In his book History of the Transport of the E.E.F Badcock mentions the care of animals including the camels, and despite what many might think, it was not only the British who had a poor understanding of these beasts which would carry heavy loads for 21 out of 25 hours. The native population also misunderstood the animals somewhat.

One of the greatest misconceptions was the idea that camels did not need water or if they did, only a sip every few days. Totally false of course, Badcock mentioned that trained camels can go around 3 days without water but like the men, they should be watered every day possible. Not always possible in war but vital that it was understood.

Today, we take roads for granted most of the time, but the roads used by both sides in the Middle East were something different altogether with many roads across the desert landscape being no more than dirt tracks or at best surfaced with rubble. Camels and donkeys could move across almost any terrain but a convoy of Motorised transport was a very much different deal entirely.

Roads often had metal reinforcement to support heavy vehicles but even that would not always be enough, especially for a column on the move. Things were made even more difficult as the Turks destroyed road and railway lines as they retreated. Across the Sinai, functional roads were made by laying down wire rabbit netting on to the soft sand.

Of course it sank when a vehicle went over it, but it was good enough to allow cars and ambulances to pass. Guy Dawnay actually calculated that without the road, ten miles over Sinai sand is equal to 25 miles anywhere else from the point of view of sheer physical effort alone, to say nothing of the lack of water, fuel and shade, and the heat. The animals also struggled, some more than others; horses in particular were unable to move at more than four kilometres an hour in such terrain.

One note in the archive mentions 180 3 ton lorries concentrated at Kantara. 180 could enable two supply columns of 96 lorries in each.. Yes the sums don't add up, but that is what the report says. These columns would be capable of feeding two mounted divisions of four brigades and divisional troops each.

It then goes on to say that this might be very difficult due to the narrow road and such larger numbers.

It was not only vehicles and camels that travelled along the roads, it was boots as well. Soldiers had to march across the sand and anyone who has walked along a beach will know how difficult it can be to walk on soft fine dry sand without sinking.

Now imagine hundreds of men loaded with equipment doing the same. Wire netting again came to the rescue, helping to make the lives of marching troops a little easier. Laid both as roads and wrapped around their feet.

It was only after the crossing of the Sinai desert that motor transport came into its own in Palestine, the Desert being far too soft to support the heavy lorries and vehicles. The increased mobility provided by mechanical transport meant that the army could cover greater distances and operate much further from the Railheads that provided the much needed supplies.

RETROSPECT

# DAMASCUS

*I made my first acquaintance with Damascus in the early days of October 1918. The place was in an unholy mess. The narrow river which runs through parts of the city was full of human and animal corpses. The Turks and Germans had had a hell of a scrap amongst themselves and I hope never again to see such a scene of desolation as I chanced upon in a Turkish Hospital.*

Damascus had been in Ottoman hands since 1516, only being lost to Ibrahim Pasha of Egypt for a few years in the 1830's. Today the City is the capital of Syria and is regarded as one of the oldest continuously inhabited cities in the World. An important City at the time, reaching Damascus meant that the Allies were pushing ever closer to forcing Ottoman forces back to Constantinople.

The Capture of Damascus (1st October 1918) was another major turning point, not only in the Sinai & Palestine Campaign but also for politics in the region and the war. It was a battle in which Cavalry played an important role under the direct command of Lieutenant General Harry Chauvel.

My (Badcocks) Ludhiana clerk in the foreground.

A short halt coming down from RISKAK- Qhalat Tappa

British and Arab forces encircled the City and defeated the combined German and Turkish forces there. It is easy to forget that German forces played a large part in this Theatre of War. In fact in 1917 & 1918, the Ottoman Army was under the command of General Erich von Falkenhayn and Otto Liman von Sanders of the German Army.

Sanders was also in command of forces at Gallipoli. Taking Damascus was not only a great military victory, effectively removing enemy forces from the area, but was also a major political & tactical achievement. After the fighting ceased, British, French and Arab forces (under Prince Faisal) all vied to get the best deal and ensure previous agreements were honoured.

British Empire troops were actually responsible for the capture of Damascus, the Light Horse Brigade in particular, but for political reasons, the Arab forces had to be seen to take the victory to make it appear they had driven out the Turks.

Consequently British forces had to remain outside the City pending the arrival of the Arabs. The City had already elected an Arab Governor before the Turks were expelled but there was still trouble on the streets. General Chauvel, whose troops captured the City, heard of the chaos and despite Lawrence's wish for the British to be seen as Allies not conquerors, had little choice but to march through the City as a show of force on 2nd October. This included representation from almost every unit under his command, with guns, armoured cars and everything in between. Supposedly the march began at 12:30 and finished at 15:00.

Shortly after the capture of Damascus on the 3rd October, a meeting took place between Allenby, Lawrence and Prince Faisal to explain what was about to happen. Since there were still hostilities in the area, supreme control would remain with the C in C meaning all military and administrative decisions would be Allenby's.

He also informed Faisal about the plan for a French Mandate in Lebanon, something which Faisal fiercely disputed, claiming to have been promised control of all Syria with access to the Mediterranean Sea. He also declined the offer of a French Liaison Officer and recognition of French guidance.

*Installed, in what had been the German Officers Club only a few hours earlier. I found an old friend of mine. Colonel Frank Stirling, Lawrence's right hand man (Lawrence's Chief of Staff in 1918 a Major at the time).*

*He kindly loaned me the services of one of his Arab interpreters and the pair of us went to see if anything could be bought at the local Harrods in the sinks etc line for which Damascus was renowned.*

*We were successful, but when the Syrian Manager, who spoke a little English, totalled up my account, I found it came to more than I had Egyptian notes to pay for, so I told him I would have to do without one or two articles I'd originally included.*

*At once he intervened saying pay me by cheque Sir" I told him my cheque book was miles away at my headquarters camp, near Ludd, in Palestine.*

*"Very good, Sir" continued the little Syrian,*

*"I give you the account and you send a cheque to my brother in Cairo, who has a shop like mine opposite Shepherds Hotel. I expect he is still there, but I have not heard for 4 years since War began."*

*I was taken aback by such trustfulness and interjected," "but how do you know that I shall pay"?*

*The little Syrian stood, metaphorically, to attention, looked me straight in the face said, "Sir! You are a British Officer."*

*I thanked him and asked whether he had done this already for others.*

*Yes! He told me he had and then produced a notebook containing many names with details, including amounts. As I glanced through the pages I realised some hundreds of pounds were involved,*

*It made me think. "Look here, I said "if you will let me have a copy of this list I will see that it reaches your brother in Cairo and when next I am there, perhaps in two months time, I will call and see him and should any of these accounts not have been paid I will do what I can to help"*

*He did as I asked, and some weeks later, when in Cairo, I made my promised call.*

*Everyone of those accounts had been paid, and, had I wished, I could have had anything in that Cairo emporium free of charge. In those days "Ciris Britannicus sum" was indeed a proud boast.*

Ciris Britannicus sum - I am (a) British Citizen, a boast that today may well see a different reaction in many parts of the world. Here though, it is important to remember that the world was a different place and this was a different time.

Badcock writes about the exchange in The History of the Transport Service of the E.E.F. but gives more details about the preceding events where he wanders through the city, following the narrow streets, the purlieus of the prostitutes quarter that was overflowing with *'flotsam and jetsam of humanity'*.

In the 1965 letter exchange with Ince, they discuss Pax Britanica (British Peace), a time 1815-1914 when the world was essentially at peace as the British ruled with no real rival, taking on the role of world police.

The topic they are discussing is the independence of Rhodesia under Ian Smith but leads on to a bigger question and an interesting point. These men had lived through a time where Britain had gone from global superpower with no one power able to challenge her, to a small insignificant island off the coast of Europe.

Aside from this view, I personally find the idea of a shopping trip in a War Zone an interesting way to spend the time in a newly captured City.

Unlike conflicts today in the same region, the likelihood of insurgents was low; it was a time of armies marching under the flag for the most part and a land glad to be free of Ottoman rule. The fact that a local businessman would trust so many British Officers on account, is clearly testament to the high regard in which they were held. Of course the concept of shops giving credit was not new; settling your account at the end of the month would be commonplace in many shops throughout Britain - but in a War Zone with a victorious Army?

As well as this legitimate purchase there were of course war trophies, one of Badcocks was offered to him by Lawrences men, namely a large bell from a railway station, likely Muslimiyeh Junction, 10 miles North of Aleppo.

A letter says it is very heavy and sits on an 8ft pedestal. He was trying to give it way in 1965 to the new National Army Museum archive or Corps Museum but no one seems to know where it ended up. Nor how he brought it back.

This captured bell is also very symbolic- *"it marked the end of the 1918 hunt in Palestine and Syria etc after Han & TURK – a distance approx that of London- Aberdeen! And though I say it who shouldn't- a hunt made possible almost entirely due to what our MT people did- Allenby appreciated that fact."* Not particularly modest but he was sure that Motorised transport had changed the style of war.

For many serving troops, home comforts were few and far between. Unlike those serving on the Western Front, Home Leave, including that of junior Officers was non-existent as it was for the ANZAC and Indian troops serving alongside them.

The closest thing were the Leave Camps set up in Egypt around Cairo and Alexandria. These camps included cinemas, theatre shows and concerts together with the vices that one could associate with an army on Campaign.

To those in Europe, rest or leave would mean a change of location and not environment. Whilst those of the EEF may have had a change of location but certainly not environment, they still had to deal with the harsh desert sun or torrential rain and mud. Although once in Palestine they did manage to arrange a cricket match or two.

The Western Front and its offensives also had a direct impact of the E.E.F. as battle hardened troops were pulled away at strategic moments to support the slog of trench warfare in France, slowing down the Allied advances across the desert.

Due to the relatively low casualty rate, Officers and NCOs in the E.E.F. were not being constantly replaced and they were able to build a much stronger relationship with the men they commanded and a practical understanding of what was possible. Most of the men were also in good physical condition, so that when they were redeployed to the Western or other Fronts, these experienced veterans proved themselves to be amongst the best troops.

In fact all front and theatres began to develop their own training manuals, though those from the Western Front became the most often used.

*The Sinai desert and southern Palestine had many interesting inhabitants apart from human beings.*

*On one occasion, round about May 1917, when returning to Cairo from East Force Headquarters, then at Asir el Belah, South of Gaza, by train to Kantara, and thence, again by train, to Cairo, I was asked by Maurice Portal (Remounts branch) to take a consignment of desert mice, scorpions, snakes etc. to the Cairo Zoo, for whom he had collected this mixed bag "They'll be all right" he said "they'll be there in 12 hours and won't need any feeding."*

*So I meekly agreed to act as courier. Unfortunately we had not legislated for a Khamsin! (Sandstorm) We had one all right. The rails were buried in sand. The engine was stuck, so were we, and the journey took 30 hours.*

*I conjured up visions of the mice eating holes into the cardboard boxes containing the snakes and the whole tribe "going Large" in the railway coach.*

*Luckily, that did not happen, but I was relieved when I had handed over my cargo to the Superintendent of the Cairo Zoo.*

*Maurice Portal(Remounts), with two other distinguished soldier-naturalists - Meinertzhagen (Intelligence)and Buxton, made a remarkable collection later on of many wild birds on the Spring and Autumn migration. Lord Allenby allowed them the services of a trooper in the City of London Yeomanry whose occupation in civilian life was with Rowland Ward of Piccadilly (Taxidermist).*

*I am not sure, but I have an idea that this collection finally found its way to the Natural History Museum in London.*

There is so much more to war than battle and bloodshed, often there are times of innovation and discovery! The idea of travelling for 30 hours with mice and snakes in cardboard boxes and the thought of what could happen, would certainly make you think twice before agreeing, but needs must!

Allenby was known for wanting to establish a firm foundation for everything around him. A very keen naturalist, it was also normal for him to bring in experts on town planning and railway engineering as it was to call in experts on the flora and fauna of the lands around him.

Badcock provided an Indian trooper and a few riding camels to assist in the efforts of Portal and Meinertzhagen. The collection he mentions again seems not to of ended up at the Natural history museum or at least the records no longer exist.

# RETROSPECT

# JERSUSALM

Lord Allenby motored vast Distances on the mostly appalling roads we had to contend with. He used a Rolls, and one of his A.D.C. usually preceded him in a German Mercedes (a captured one!). One would see a sort of dust storm approaching in a series of bounds like a tennis ball as the driver of the Mercedes did his best to keep well ahead of the chiefs car to prevent any hold up.

The Chief had a first class driver, one Brennan of the Army Service Corps. I was talking to him one day, when, clad in shorts, he was cleaning the Chief's car.

I noticed his back round his shoulders seemed a curious black and yellow colour and enquired the cause.

He then explained that whenever the Chief, who sat always in the back of his Rolls, wanted him to stop, or to turn to the right, or the left, he brought the handle of his stick, like a Mahout using his elephant driving-goad, on to the appropriate portion of his back.

As harsh and abusive as this might sound, with the roar of the engine making conversation difficult it seems quite a logical step to try and make things easier and ensure that the reaction was fast and the instruction not lost to the wind –

> *Man-power problems became acute at times and one suggestion put forward was the low-medical category men could well be used to drive motor lorries which in those days had solid rubber tyres and open cabs. (the German lorries had steel tyres!). Fortunately for those who ran the M.T. of the E.E.F. this idea did not prevail for long, for the leading advocates of this heretical policy were collected one scorching hot day and put aboard an MT convoy from Jerusalem to Jericho and back. As distance went, there wasn't much in it, a mere 25 miles each way; but Jerusalem was 3,000 ft above sea level and Jericho, 1200 ft below, but the dust along those 25 miles had to be experienced to be believed. It was truly diabolical, and it ended all further ideas of all and sundry being physically compliant to drive heavy lorries in Palestine in the heat of summer or the torrential rains of winter.*

By the time of the Third Battle of Gaza (1st & 2nd November 1917) the rail network was comparable to that of Western Europe, so that travel over the long distance from Egypt had been greatly improved and even terminated close to the Front Line. Following the capture of Beersheba the track was swiftly extended in order that supplies could be easily unloaded and sent by road to Jerusalem.

*You nevertheless found in the vicinity of the good Samaritans hut, along this self-same Jerusalem-Jericho road, an ancient monastery, surrounded by barren rock, yet fed with water in a small shallow aqueduct, which enabled a grape vine to grow luxuriantly and produce superb white grapes. What a contrast!*

*The wild spring flowers on the plain of Sharon and in the Judean hills were a wonderful sight and my final picture of those unforgettable days in an historic land is of Lord Allenby, on a hillside on the Jerusalem-Latrun road, picking those beautiful wild Red Anemones and waving a bunch in acknowledgement to your salute as you motored past him.*

Like many events in War, the capture of Jerusalem was not simply a one-piece set battle, event or engagement, but was rather a complex mix of battle, actions, offensives and defence.

The battle for Jerusalem took place between 17th November - 31st December 1917 and extended from North of Jaffa (captured by the British on 17th November) right up into the Judean hills. The Prime Minister (David Lloyd George - the Welsh Wizard) described the capture as a 'Christmas present for the British people'.

Amusingly the Mayor of Jerusalem attempted to give the letter of surrender from the Ottoman Governor to two sergeants who were scouting ahead of the main force. Sergeant James Sedgewick and Frederick Hurcomb of 2/19th Battalion, London Regiment refused to take the surrender. Instead it was finally accepted by Brigadier General C.F. Waston.

Allenby famously entered the city on foot as a mark of respect, two days after the Official Surrender by the Jaffa gate. Kaiser Wilhelm II on the other hand, visited the Holy City in 1898 with all the pomp and circumstance he could muster..

Allenby was accompanied by various troops on this ceremonial entry to the City, including units from the Light Horse & New Zealand Mounted Rifles Brigades. It was a symbolic entrance of a Christian Nation capturing the Sacred City from the Muslem for the first time in hundreds of years.

The Battle for the region was hard as the terrain lent itself to defensive fighting, something the retreating Turkish & German troops used to their advantage.

They were still pushed back allowing the British to establish a new and strong strategic line. Following the capture of Jerusalem, the British did not have it easy and they had to defend the hard won City until the line advanced in September, 1918 towards Damascus and Aleppo.

Supplies and transport in this offensive were vitally important and somewhat challenging since much of the Offensive took place far from supply bases and railheads. As the Ottoman Forces retreated they exacerbated the problems by destroying much of the existing infrastructure – already in a parlous state.

Leaving the British forces to quite literally soldier on.

British forces never reached the Ottoman capital of Istanbul, instead the Armistice of Mudros was signed ending the war in the Middle East on the 30th October 1918.

The war may have ended but it changed the region forever.

Indian Trooper

Some of Badcock's Men dancing on Xmas Day- Khanaqin

RETROSPECT

# AFTERWORD

There you have it – Retrospect - from the English Home Counties to the rocky shores of Gallipoli, across the dusty plains of Egypt and on to the cities of Jerusalem and Damascus.

I hope you have enjoyed this, at some times, humorous journey though the War such a long way from the Western Front.

The Sinai and Palestine campaign changed the Middle East and the World forever. What followed during the Mandate Period created new Nations and borders in the region, the effects of which are with us today.

This book is simply a record of one man's time in the War. There are many good books, articles and websites that look at the Campaign in depth and provide an analysis of the different battles that took place. I suggest that anyone who has even the slightest interest in history take a look.

I hesitate to suggest specific titles but there is a wealth of information available on-line including Facebook Groups and Blogs. Many of these are not mainstream and take a bit of finding but the people, places and events described in Badcock's account should give you a starting point.

Why has this Front been so overlooked by many? Well as suggested, this Campaign dealt in the thousands, not millions.

# RETROSPECT

For many, even at the time, it was seen as a side-show or picnic to the main event and it seems sad that this has not changed in the public eye.

Many of the troops deployed were ANZAC forces but there were thousands of men from Britain who served alongside their colonial cousins and large numbers of troops from other Nations within the British Empire. Popular media shapes how we view the past and this tends to focus on the Pals and the trenches of Europe which were undoubtedly a "hell of a place". Yet so was the desert, scorching hot days and freezing nights.

Retrospect simply highlights a small part of the struggle that took place between 1914-1918 across the Globe and although it was not the War to end all Wars, it was certainly one that created the World we have today, in more ways than you may have thought at the beginning.

I hope you have found this book interesting and that it may have sparked your appetite to learn more about the First World War and the other Fronts and parts of the conflict you are not familiar with.

Believed to be Sir John Laycock (Nottinghamshire Royal Horse Artillery, AN-ZAC mounted Division)

# RETROSPECT

# APPENDIX

## About the Author & his world

In his own words (slightly abbreviated) and with some explanation from me, I have the pleasure to introduce Brigadier Gerald Eliot Badcock C.B.E, D.S.O taken from his book 'Two Generations'.

Gerald was born to Theophila Lowther Dumergue & General Sir Alexander Robert Badcock (who was Lord Robert's Chief Supplies and Transport Office on the march to Kabul in 1889) in Murree, India in 1883 and returned to England in 1893. (It is worth noting that Badcock's father, Sir Alexander, was a well-regarded military man of his day, featuring in the Whos Who books of the time and was Quartermaster General of India in 1895. He also took part in the famous march to Kandahar.)

"I went to school in September 1893 at Lambrook near Bracknell and stayed there till April 1897. Leaving there, I went in May 1897 to Wellington College.

From Wellington I went to Pembroke College Cambridge in October 1901 with the intention of being a Doctor! I even succeeded in passing one part of the first M.B examination!

But in the spring of 1903 Father was very ill and I knew he was worried about my future. So at the beginning of May of that year, I sat down to work for the University Candidates' Entrance Examination for the Army. I only had seven weeks in which to work up for it - only fourteen vacancies were to be given and there were over a hundred candidates; however I was lucky enough to pass - No.13!

The following March (1904) I had to take the Military Subjects part of the further examination and got through fifth in order of merit. "On June 4, 1904, I got my Commission as a 2nd Lieutenant in the Army Service Corps (ASC). I joined the A.S.C. at Woolwich in July 1904. "

To give you a picture of the man he was 5ft.11" when he enlisted and was married in 1908 at the age of 25.

Three weeks later, fourteen officers, including myself, out of some twenty-five in our Mess, got scarlet fever (incidentally, two died). In September 1904, when I had recovered, I was sent to the A.S.C. Depot at Longford, in Ireland."

From 1904-1913 Badcock spent his time between Ireland and Aldershot. Most of his writing about that time focuses on a selective variety of topics - cricket & hunting which as we will see left a lasting impression on him.

"In 1913, I rejoined the A.S.C. Training establishment (of which the Depot I'd served in from 1905-9 was part). On August 4, 1914, on the outbreak of the Great War, I became Adjutant of the R.A.S.C. Training Establishment."

The role of an Adjutant is a military officer who acts as an administrative assistant to a senior officer.

"I left in February 1915 and went out as D.A.D.T (Deputy Assistant Director of Transport) to Gallipoli. In October 1915 I became A.D.T. and held that post, which carried the temporary rank of Lieutenant-Colonel, till February 1919, when I came back to England, after serving in Gallipoli, Egypt, Palestine, and Syria."

The list of countries above is where the action of Retrospect takes place and in this book, Badcock touches little on this part of his life. He does however take the time to thank and name two Officers he served under.

"I was very lucky in the War for I never missed a day's work for four years, either through sickness or wounds, and one way and another I came into contact with the opportunities to acquire acquaintance with each. Also I was more than lucky in my two immediate Chiefs: Major General F. W. Koe, 1916-16 and Major General G.F. Davies, 1916-19, as you can see from what they got for me in the way of rewards- C.B.E (1919); Brevet Lieutenant-Colonelcy (1918): D.S.O. (1917); and four mentions in dispatches."

"From February to May 1919 I commanded a Mechanical Transport Depot at Kempton Park and then went to Q.M.G.3 branch in the War Office till January 1922."

The Q.M.G.3 branch of the War Office was the branch responsible for Military transport, similar branches were Q.M.G.6 which was responsible for supplies.

"A three-months' course followed at the now defunct School of Administration at Chisledon, in Wilts, and then in May 1922 I went to Bermuda as O.C., R.A.S.C., where we stayed till March 1925. Whilst there I had two spells in 1922 and in 1923 as Acting Governor."

Bermuda, the wonderfully beautiful island in the North Atlantic has a long history with Britain, becoming a formal colony in 1707 and is still today a British Overseas Territory. Although sounding like some sort of sunny holiday, Bermuda plays an important part of Badcock's story when it comes to Retrospect.

Whilst there with his young children, he first recorded his experiences of the War in his book- A History of the Transport Services of The Egyptian Expeditionary Force 1916-18. It is interesting to note that this book was written in the 1920s whilst Retrospect, a more personal account dates from the later 1950s.

Although the book received strong reviews and contained a preface from Field Marshall Viscount Allenby, G.C.B., G.C.M.G. ; sales, alas, did not boom.

"Actually the reviews – at home, in India, in Australia and in Egypt—were really eulogistic! I only wish the sales had been on the same high level! In 1925 I had 1000 copies printed, of which 500 were bound in book form. By 1933 a total of 331 copies has been disposed of, that is to say, sold, given away, etc.

The sale price(s) was 21s. (approx. £1 not adjusting for inflation) of which I got 14s., the other 7s. being taken by the publishers! Why, I don't quite know, for I paid for the cost of printing; however, there is a certain amount of satisfaction in having pieced together one's experiences in book form."

Despite these poor sales, Badcock, literally, soldiered on.

"In April 1927, I got packed off at seven days' notice to China, of all places!--- it was the year of the Chinese troubles. However, I got back home by January 1928 and went back to my old job at Bordon till early in February 1929, when I became Chief Instructor at the R.A.S.C. training establishment at Aldershot. I held this normal three-year appointment for just over two, as the 'practical joke' or 'fairy godmother' department, whichever you will!

The War Office decided to make me a substantive Colonel by jumping me up from the rank of Major, by virtually leaving out the intervening rank of Lieutenant-Colonel and finally sending me on May 8, 1931, to be an Instructor at The Senior Officers' School at Sheerness: here I remained till December 31, 1933, and on January 1, 1934, I again had the luck to get another first-class appointment as an A.Q.M.G. at the War Office. So there in brief is my thirty years of soldiering...."

The story did not end there. Following retirement in 1936, he was recalled to the military to serve during WW2 as Director of Salvage. This included the organisation and administration of Army Salvage both in the UK and in all overseas theatres of war.

His obituary in The Waggoner in 1966 states "The Corps loses one of it most colourful and distinguished sons"

**Service Record**

1904: Commissioned 2 Lt. Army Service Corps

1909-1912: Adjutant A.S.C. Curragh

1914: Adjutant A.S.C. Aldershot

1915-1919: Deputy Assistant and Assistant Director of Transport Gallipoli, Egypt, Palestine, Syria

1919-1922: War Office.

1922-1925: O.C. R.A.S.C. Bermuda

1925-1926: O.C. R.A.S.C. Bordon

1927: O.C. R.A.S.C., Independent Brigade China.

1929-1931- Chief Instructor, Senior Officers School, Sheerness.

1934 to 1936: Assistant Quartermaster-General, (Movements) War Office and responsible for all moves by land and sea of the British Army in peace and war.

1936: April- retired from Army

1939-Recalled

1940-1944- Director of Salvage, War Office.

1944- Retired

**Awards:**

D.S.O. 1917

C.B.E. 1919

Brevet Lt. Colonel 1918.

4 mentions in dispatches

Promoted to Substantive Colonel (1931) from the rank of Major.

Experience: 30 years in all kinds of Military food supplies- including petrol, contracts. All forms of transport- Camel, Donkey, Mechanical Transport, Rail and Sea.

Believed to be Sir John Laycock

## ARMY SERVICE CORPS

An army marches on its stomach, travels on its boots and beds down with blankets, none of which would be possible without the logistical support provided by the Army Service Corps (A.S.C). In modern times we know it as The Royal Logistics Corps which was formed in 1993 as a union of a number of Corps.

As you might imagine the British Army has a long history of needing support in making campaigns happen and for a long time this support came from civilians.

The first uniformed transport corps formed in 1794, known as the Royal Waggoners. They were short lived and were soon disbanded. As time passed there were various incarnations of this important support network as the boots of the British Soldiers were followed around the world by wagons, carts, mules and donkeys, making an Empire possible.

Not until 1888 was the Army Service Corps established as a unit in its own right, although the importance of civilian involvement continued.

The prefix "Royal" was added to the Army Service Corps in 1918 for services during WW1. You will notice in the "about the author" section there is a change from A.C.S. to R.A.C.S.

The history of this important part of the Army is fascinating and alone among the 'service' corps, its personnel are considered combatants. If this is of interest to the reader, I suggest further investigation of the Corps history, either by a quick google or reading one of the many books or articles on the subject.

Badcock's experience during WW1 took place whilst serving wholly in the A.S.C., a Corps that went from 6,500 men at the start of the war, to 325,000 by 1918. Of that number, by 1918 74,924 served in the Egyptian Expeditionary Force (E.E.F.)

These numbers were made up of men from across the globe, British, ANZAC, Indians & Egyptians.

Transport for the army at the time was made up of anything that came to hand able to carry men and supplies to wherever they needed to be - everything from trains, planes, ships, motorised transport, donkeys, asses, mules, camels and the men themselves. These Transports were divided into four branches - Mechanical transport, Horse transport, Supply and Camel transport.

Mechanical/Motorised transport, car, trucks & lorries were still a relatively new concept at the time.

To put it into context, Ford began production of its famous Model T in 1908, only 6 years before the start of the War and Tanks were not deployed until 1916. The use of trucks and cars meant that far more could be transported over greater distances, taking less manpower and, in theory, saving time!

The E.E.F had around 467,650 men and was maintained by a slightly lesser army of 74,800 horses, 39,100 mules, 35,000-40,000 camels and 11,000 donkeys, all of which, needed feeding and watering. It also had a fleet of 1,703 motor lorries, 1467 cars & vans, 530 ambulances, 1,487 motorcycles and 374 tractors and tractor trucks - not to mention the numbers of boats, ships and trains backing it up.

In the terrain faced by the E.E.F. many of the so called "roads" were simply impassable by trucks and cars, especially in the Middle East where pack animals still prevailed and the narrow mountain passes were not wide enough for vehicles to get through. Even on the Western Front, horses were still used to pull heavy guns and transports.

Towards the end of the War, more and more lorries were converted to run on rails to help make up for a shortfall in rolling stock. One lorry for example, with three 10 ton trucks in tow could move up to 33 tons of supplies - everything from food, water, ammunition, uniform - whatever was required.

Many cars we know today were used by the Army. Ford, Mercedes, Studebaker and Rolls Royce were used by both sides. Each vehicle had its own strengths and weaknesses. Fords cylinders wore quickly, with the help of sand and dust.

The cure - widening of the piston grooves. Boring as this might be, it was vitally important.

As deputy Director of Transport, this was something all too familiar to Badcock who had to find the best method of transport for the job and deal with these hostile conditions, from sun baked deserts to snow covered mountain passes.

The E.E.F. was effectively cut off from Britain when it came to supplies. The submarine threat meant that supplies from the homeland were few and far between. Although Badcock's role was more about transport, he would have known only too well of the situation. However a large percentage of mostly frozen or preserved meat from the Argentine managed to survive the voyage, with other supplies coming in from across the Empire.

The Deputy Quartermaster General - Major General Walter Campbell, Allenby's Chief Executive Officer, was the man charged with resolving the supply problem.

He set up vast fishing fleets on Lake Manzala (west of Port

Said). Egypt provided fresh vegetables, hay and more and following the capture of Jaffa in November 1917, the British Forces also had effectively, an unlimited supply of oranges. Something Badcock took advantage of, having at least one a day between November 1917 till mid-June 1918.

## THE ARMY SERVICE CORPS

There's a handful of men in the army,
Who seldom shoulder a gun,
And its little that's known about them,

When everything's said and done;
And they try to escape any notice,
As they quietly slip off to War,
For they never expect a send-off,
In the Army Service Corps.

They don't aim at capturing prisoners,
Or at taking the enemy's flag,
But they serve in a humbler vocation,
For the sake of the Grand Old Rag;
Amid the inferno of battle,
And in Spite of the cannon's roar,
They keep on quietly working,
In the Army Service Corps.

When the foeman's heavy gun-fire,
Has scattered and smashed their supplies,
They take good grip on their upper lips,
And with "never-say-die" in their eyes,
They hustle around and square things up,
And put them in order once more.
For they don't know the meaning of quitting,
In the Army Service Corps.

RETROSPECT

When their fellow-soldiers are resting,
Awaiting a new day's dawn,
They are desperately heaving and straining
With muscle and sinew and brawn,
For they must deliver the rations,
Although they are weary and sore-
They are ripping good men that can stick it.
In the Army Service Corps.

And when the war is over,
And peace again doth reign,
This handful of men silently turn,
Back to their homes once again;
And they try to escape any notice,
As they quietly slip ashore,
But it's a way they have of doing things,
In the Army Service Corps.

(Poem from Badcock's Papers)

## OTHER CAMPAIGNS

The War in Africa was fought throughout the colonies Germany had managed to acquire in a relatively short space of time. The campaigns in these areas were over quite quickly save for that of German East Africa, where fighting still continued after the Armistice had been signed.

Fighting in Mesopotamia took place in what is now modern Iraq, which the Ottomans had largely controlled since the 16th century, although never enjoying full control. When War broke out in Europe, British forces were sent to protect oil fields in the area. The Indian Expeditionary Force D was deployed and fought across the territory for the duration of the War. Following various failures such as the Siege of Kut (7th December 1915 - 29th April 1916) 1917 saw a change of fortune for British troops with the capture of Baghdad in March 1917 and the capture of the Berlin-Baghdad railway. As with the Sinai & Palestine Campaign, troops experienced a huge range of temperatures with a high of 48 degrees being common, disease was rife, leading to increased casualties.

# OTTOMAN EMPIRE

The Ottoman Empire, often regarded as the 'sick man of Europe' in the early 20th Century, was founded in 1299. At its height it controlled the majority of North Africa, large parts of Greece and Eastern Europe all the way across to modern Iran.

By the time of WW1 it was greatly reduced and now comprised only Anatolia and parts of Mesopotamia down through Palestine and onwards towards Aden. Still a vast size but nothing compared to its former glory despite attempts to make it so. This even extended to receiving a military mission and advisors from Germany.

Prior to WW1, the Ottoman Empire had been fighting a series of wars (commonly known as the Balkan Wars) with its Eastern European neighbours and other traditional enemies, with the support of Austria Hungary. The fighting in 1912 & 1913 left it sorely depleted of resources and funds.

The years of expansion were long gone and the economy was now based around agriculture, unlike those it was about to fight which had benefited from industrialisation and subsequent growth.

Both the Allies and the Central powers initially tried to gain the support of the Ottoman Empire, however the Allies were allied to Russia, the Turks long term enemy, so only one choice remained.

On the 29th October 1914, the Ottomans attacked Russian ports in the Black Sea in support of their allies. This Northern Front was vital to the Ottomans who saw it as an opportunity to gain large amounts of territory.

For the duration of the War, the Ottoman or Turkish High Command was based in Constantinople (Istanbul) placing it a long way from the action on many fronts. With the internal infrastructure of the country in chaos, transport to the Front took far longer longer than in most other countries engaged in the War, causing delays not only in the receipt of military orders but also supplies and other vital resources.

Following its defeat, the Ottoman Empire was occupied and divided up by the Allies with the Treaty of Sevres 1920. The Treaty was short lived and unrest caused the Turkish War of Independence (1919-1923). The cessation of hostilities resulted in a new Treaty - the Treaty of Lausanne – which was instrumental in the decision made by the International Committee to recognise modern Turkey.

# RETROSPECT

# **TIMELINE**

**1914**

4th August
*Britain Declares War on Germany*

18th October
*First Battle of Ypres (France)*

29th October
*Turkey enters WW1 on Germany's side*

**1915**

Early February
*Badcock deployed on Gallipoli Campaign*

22nd February
*Gallipoli Campaign Begins*

22nd April
*Second Battle of Ypres (France)*

25th April
*First landings at Gallipoli- including Cape Helles and ANZAC*

9th July
*German forces in South West Africa Surrender*

July
*V.I.P visit Gallipoli*

6th August
*The ANZAC Summer Offensive starts*

14th October
*General Hamilton was replaced by General Sir Charles Monro as CIC of the Gallipoli Campaign*

31st October
*Monro advises Field Marshal Herbert Kitchener that Allied troops should withdraw from Gallipoli. Kitchener does not agree*

22nd November
*Kitchener finally agrees to the evacuation of Gallipoli*

19th December
*Evacuation of Gallipoli starts*

## 1916

January
*Conscription into British Army introduced*

8th/9th January
*Evacuation of Cape Helles, Gallipoli*

21st February
*Battle of Verdun starts (France)*

24th-29th April
*Easter Rising in Ireland*

31st May- 1st June
*Battle of Jutland- coast of Denmark*

1st July
*Battle of the Somme begins*

1917
8th-11 March
*The British Capture Baghdad*

15th March
*Russian Revolution begins*

6th April
*USA declares War on Germany*

17th-19th April
*Second Battle of Gaza*

May
*Badcock returns to Cairo from East Fore Headquarters near Asir el Belah*

27th June
*General Sir Edmund Allenby arrives in Egypt to relieve Sir Archibald Murray and takes command of the E.E.F.*

31st July- 6th November
*Battle of Passchendaele/Third Battle of Ypres begins (France)*

September
*Badcock is at El Fukhari- General Chetwode's Headquarters*

31st October
*Battle of Beersheba takes place*

1st-2nd November
*Third Battle of Gaza*

9th December
*Capture of Jerusalem*

11th December
*Allenby enters Jerusalem*

## 1918

8-11th August
*Battle of Amiens- Western Front*

September
*Final Conference of General Allenby with Corps Commander*

1st October
*Capture of Damascus & Beirut*
*Badcock arrived in Damascus*

30th October
*Armistice of Mudros - End of the War between the Ottoman Empire & Allies*

11th November
*End of WW1, the Armistice was signed in Redonthes, France*

10th December
*Surafend Affair*

## BADCOCK'S NARRATIVE OF EVENTS FROM 24TH APRIL 1915 - LANDING ON W. BEACH

April 24th - Transport and warships rendezvoused at TENEDOS, sailed at 10 p.m. and going dead slow arrived off Cape HELLES about 4 a.m.

15th - (assumed to be 25th) Covering part immediately transferred to ships boats in the dark- boats towed by trawlers and pinnaces in strings of six.

5 a.m. First gun from the AMETHYST. Warships escorting 6 tows each about 2 miles from the shore moved slowly forwards firing from bow guns, in "line abreast". A rather hazy dawn and the smoke from the bursting shells soon obscured targets.

6 a.m. Very heavy bombardment. The tows have now got well ahead.

6.3. a.m. Boats cast off from their trawlers etc., and start rowing, 30 soldiers in each boat, with a crew of 10. Heavy rifle and machine gun fire from shore.

6.5. a.m. Escorting warships steam close in and open fire with 6" and 8" guns.

Lancashire Fusiliers have landed and found the beach covered with barbed wire - suffer very severely from rifle and machine gun fire - all men trying to cut wire are shot.

Remainder get through gaps with magnificent dash and find what cover they can under cliffs for a moment's rest. Men have landed up to their waists in water- many hit in the boats on their way in- most have to bob down to their necks in the water to avoid bullets.

6.25 a.m. A dash up the cliff on the left gives the regiment a footing on the top.

6.40 a.m. Second line of tows arrive off the beach, met by heavy fire from shore. Boats of first tow seen struggling to get back, some with only one or two of the crew fit to pull an oar.

6.45 am. Ridge on right of beach occupied. Dash across the ridge on the left results in capture of first Turkish trenches.

7.30 am. High ground round beach on one hand, but troops still exposed to heavy rifle fire.

Remainder get through gaps with magnificent dash and find what ?
9.30 am. Landing on all beaches except V reported correct. Wounded begin to return to the ship.

11.30 am. Landed at W beach. Situation serious perimeter of ridge being held, and no more, by 2 ½ battalions (Essex, Lancs and ½ Hants) all of which had suffered severely. Reinforced by 5 p.m. by 5th Royal Scots. Firing down except for Y beach where it was kept up all night.

Midnight. Determined counter attack launched by the Turks. Heavy firing all night. Situation again critical, but men do not give way a foot, although worn out, unsupported, and the last reserves used up.

26th- Fire kept up till 4 p.m. after which comparatively quiet. Learned that landing at V beach has not been successful. Dublin Fusiliers and Munsters had suffered severely while still in the boats, losing nearly half their numbers. 3.30 p.m. they force a landing,take the "Old Castle" and the village SEDD EL BAHR (with ½ Hants Regt. This relieves pressure all along the line and the Turks retire. Quiet night and morning.

27th – Both sides worn out and disorganized. Advance again at 4.30 p.m. under shell fire but not very serious opposition. K.O.S.B. who landed on Y beach and were severely handled on night 25th-26th, re-embarked on 26th, afternoon. No transport available up to date except 30 ponies sneaked from the Mountain Battery- considerable difficulty experienced in getting ammunition and water to the firing line. My servant reported in the evening. He had been on the "RIVER CLYDE" a collier which was purposely run ashore with 2000 men on V beach but the fire was too hot to allow the men to get out of her until today.

April 28th- Troops advanced 8.30 am.- considerable opposition on slopes of AEBR BABA- check at 2.30- once more advancing about 4, when trench suddenly gave way leaving the Worcesters right flank in the air. Day ended in a gain of about a mile of country on the left, the right and centre occupying the same line as the morning. Gap between 2 lines filled up without opposition the next morning. Men are tired but cheery. Spent all day and all night running out ammunition, water and supplies to troops in the firing line. Bed at 3 am. "Zion Mule Corps" recruited from Jew refugees from Syria, arrived in the nick of time as we were getting very hard up for transport.

29th- Quite day and night. Troops reorganize and rest and dig themselves in. I return to G.H.Q.

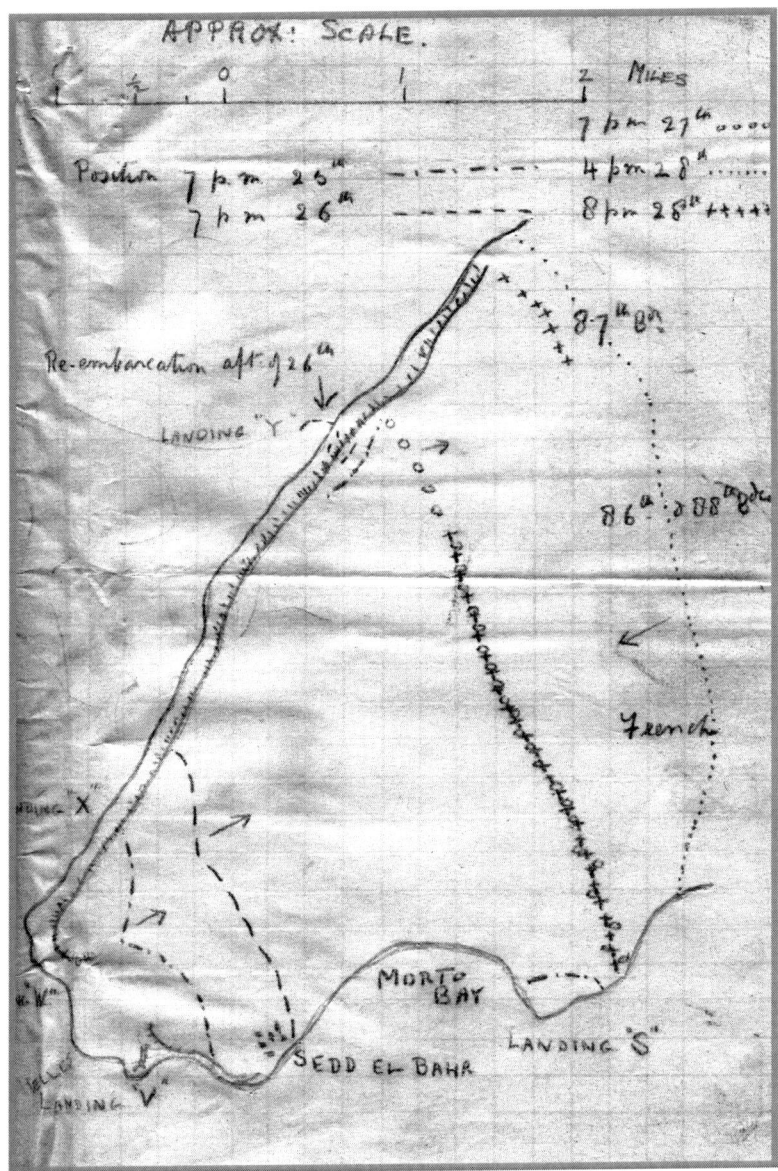

Hand drawn Map of Gallipoli Peninsular

# RETROSPECT

# BIBLIOGRAPHY

**Bruce, Anthony** (2013) The Last Crusade; The Palestine Campaign in the First World War, London, Thistle Publishing.

**Falls, Cyril** (1964) Armageddon 1918, London, Weidenfeld and Nicolson.

**Badcock, G.E.** (Unknown) TWO GENERATIONS

**Badcock, G.E.** (1925), A History of the Transport Service of the Egyptian Expeditionary Force 1916-1917-1918, London, Hug Rees

**Huges, Matthew,** (1999), Allenby and British Strategy in the Middle East 1917-1919, London, Routledge

(1966) p. 5 The Waggoner, Royal Corps of Transport (RCT) Journal

**Allenby, General Sir Edmund H.H.; T. E. Lawrence** (1919) A Brief Record of the Advance of the Egyptian Expeditionary Force. Under the Command of General Sir Edmund H.H. Allenby. London His Majesty's Stationery Office,

**Lawrence, T. E.** (1997), Seven Pillars of Wisdom, London, Wordsworth Edition

**Pedersen, Peter** (2018), ANZACS on the Western Front: The Australian War Memorial Battlefield Guide, Wiley-Blackwell